MW01243425

THE PRODIGAL SON AND OTHER PARABLES AS PLAYS

MARGARET CHEASEBRO

BROADMAN PRESS

NASHVILLE, TENNESSEE

© Copyright 1992 • Broadman Press
All rights reserved
4260-65
ISBN: 0-8054-6065-9
Dewey Decimal Classification: 812
Subject Heading: RELIGIOUS DRAMA-COLLECTIONS
Library of Congress Catalog Card Number: 92-7232

Printed in the United States of America

Library of Congress Cataloging-in-Publication Data

Cheasebro, Margaret, 1945-
    The prodigal son and other parables as plays / Margaret Cheasebro.
    p.   cm.
    Summary: A collection of plays based on parables from the Bible,
including "The Good Samaritan," "The Prodigal Son," and "Lazarus,
the Beggar."
    ISBN 0-8054-6065-9
    1. Christian drama, American. 2. Children's plays, American.
3. Jesus Christ—Parables—Adaptations. [1. Jesus Christ-
-Parables—Drama. 2. Jesus Christ—Parables—Adaptations. 3. Bible
plays. 4. Plays.] I. Title.
PS3553.H347P7   1993
812'.54—dc20
                                   92-7232
                                        CIP
                                        AC

Contents

1 The Prodigal Son
Based on Luke 15:11-32

(the depth of God's love)

CHARACTERS

JONATHAN, father
BARNABAS, attorney
JESSE, elder son
SAMUEL, younger son
AHAZ, bartender
CAIN, man in bar
LAMECH, man in bar
JEZEBEL, girl in bar
JOHN, farmer
Any number of people can play the part of pigs eating out of the feed pan

PROPS

Small plastic bag of white flour
Bucket
Big washtub for pigs to eat out of
Official-looking document to represent a will
Table with four chairs
Table that can be used for a bar
Four glasses

Act 1

(JONATHAN, BARNABAS, JESSE, *and* SAMUEL *are seated in the living room, center stage.* JONATHAN *faces* JESSE *and* SAMUEL *while* BARNABAS *sits to the right at a table with an official-looking document.)*

JONATHAN: Jesse and Samuel, you are my only children, and I want you to know how I have divided my wealth between you. Barnabas, please tell them the contents of my will.

BARNABAS: Yes, Sir. Your will divides your wealth between both sons with Jesse getting a slightly larger portion because he is the oldest.

SAMUEL (*to* JESSE): Why did you have to be born first? You have all the luck.

JESSE: Don't blame me. I didn't plan it that way.

JONATHAN: Boys, don't argue in front of our attorney. Barnabas, please draw up the final will and bring it to me to sign.

BARNABAS: Yes, sir.

(BARNABAS *exits right.*)

JONATHAN: Samuel, do you think the will is unfair?

SAMUEL: Yes I do! Jesse always gets the best of everything.

JONATHAN: That's because he is the oldest, Samuel, and he has more responsibilities than you do.

SAMUEL: But I can handle responsibility as well as he can.

JESSE: Is that why you lost twenty of our goats when you herded them last week?

SAMUEL: That wasn't my fault. A dust devil blew through the herd, scared the goats, and made them scatter.

JESSE: There was no dust devil the time you took a nap under a tree and let the cattle wander into quicksand.

SAMUEL: I was tired because you talked in your sleep the night before and kept me awake.

JONATHAN: Boys, please don't argue.

SAMUEL: I can't stand living here any more. I want to get out. Now.

JESSE: Good riddance.

SAMUEL: Father, give me my inheritance now, and I'll leave.

I'll make a success of myself and show you I'm as good as Jesse.

JONATHAN: I might just let you go. Being on your own might teach you a lot.

JESSE: You mean he gets his half of everything now?

JONATHAN: Yes.

JESSE: That's not fair.

JONATHAN: Everything that is not Samuel's will be yours, Jesse. Does that sound fair?

JESSE: I guess so.

SAMUEL: Well I want my share today. Then I'm out of here!

JONATHAN: All right. But if you change your mind, you can always come home.

(JONATHAN *and* JESSE *exit left.* SAMUEL *exits right.*)

Act 2

(SAMUEL *enters from right and swaggers to a bar at center back.* AHAZ, *the bartender, stands behind the bar. At front center is a table at which* CAIN *and* LAMECH *sit.* JEZEBEL *stands at the left end of the bar.*)

SAMUEL (*to* AHAZ): Give me a beer.

AHAZ: Coming right up.

SAMUEL: Thanks.

AHAZ: That your sports car outside?

SAMUEL: Yeah.

AHAZ: It's a beaut.

CAIN (*calls from his seat at the table*): You new in town?

SAMUEL: Yeah. Just drove in today.

LAMECH: Where you from?

SAMUEL: Down south a ways.

AHAZ: You planning to stay awhile?

SAMUEL: Maybe.

CAIN: This is a great place to live.

LAMECH: Yeah, we can show you a good time.

CAIN: All it takes is a little money.

SAMUEL: I've got plenty of that. Drinks for everyone, bartender.

CAIN (*to* LAMECH): This guy sounds loaded.

(AHAZ *puts beer in front of* CAIN, LAMECH, *and* JEZEBEL. JEZEBEL *saunters over to* SAMUEL *at the bar.*)

JEZEBEL: Hey, you're cute. I like people who share their money.

SAMUEL: What's your name?

JEZEBEL: Jezebel.

SAMUEL: Would you like to go for a ride in my sports car?

JEZEBEL: Yeah, if you take me to the biggest gambling casino around. I'll bet you're real good at gambling.

SAMUEL: Oh, uh, yeah, sure, I'm pretty good.

JEZEBEL: Let's go then.

LAMECH: Before you two go off, come here a minute.

(JEZEBEL *and* SAMUEL *go over to the table and sit down with* LAMECH *and* CAIN.)

LAMECH: Thanks for the beer. It tastes great, but I have something better.

SAMUEL: What?

(LAMECH *holds out a plastic bag full of white powder.*)

LAMECH: White stuff, baby, the pure thing.

SAMUEL: Yeah?

JEZEBEL: Take my word for it, it's the best.

CAIN: Yeah, it'll send you on a wild, crazy trip. You'll love it, man.

SAMUEL: How much?

LAMECH: For you, since you're such a good buddy, just five.

SAMUEL: Five?

CAIN: Yeah. Five hundred smackers. That's not too much for a rich dude like you, is it?

SAMUEL: Uh, no. Sure, I'll take it. What do I do with it?
LAMECH: Man, where did you come from? The back hills of Squaresville?
CAIN: You mean you never tried this stuff before?
JEZEBEL: Leave my man alone. I'll show him how to use it.
SAMUEL: Thanks.

(SAMUEL *and* JEZEBEL *stand up.*)

JEZEBEL: See you boys later. We're going gambling.

(SAMUEL *and* JEZEBEL *exit left.* SAMUEL *comes back from stage left with his clothes messed up. He walks to the bar.*)

AHAZ: What happened to you?
SAMUEL: I lost all my money gambling, and I wrecked my car.
AHAZ: Were you drunk?
SAMUEL: I guess. That white powder made me feel real crazy.
AHAZ: What happened to the girl you were with?
SAMUEL: When I lost all my money, she got interested in someone else.
AHAZ: Sounds like you had a rough time.
SAMUEL: Yeah. Give me a drink, please.
AHAZ: Do you have money to pay for it?
SAMUEL: No.
AHAZ: Then you're out of luck.

(SAMUEL *turns to* CAIN *and* LAMECH *at the table.*)

SAMUEL: Can either of you lend me money for a drink?
CAIN: Sorry, pal.
LAMECH: Not me.
SAMUEL: Some friends you turned out to be!

(SAMUEL *exits left.*)

Act 3

(At a farm by a pigpen. JOHN, *the farmer and* SAMUEL *are talking at center stage.)*

JOHN: All you have to do is slop the pigs twice a day. Think you can do it?

SAMUEL: Yeah. I used to take care of my father's animals.

JOHN: OK. Payday's every Friday. I can't pay you much.

SAMUEL: When do I start?

JOHN: Right now.

*(*JOHN *exits left.)*

SAMUEL: How did I get into this mess? I was going to be famous. Now look at me. I've got about the lowest job a man could have. If only I'd been wiser with my money.

*(*JOHN *enters left.)*

JOHN: Hey, boy, don't stand around all day dreaming. I expect my employees to work.

SAMUEL: Yes, Sir.

*(*JOHN *exits right.* SAMUEL *picks up a bucket and pours its contents into a big washtub for the pigs. Pigs eat it with a grunting sound.)*

SAMUEL: I'm so hungry, I could eat this slop. I haven't had a meal in two days. What am I going to do?

*(*JOHN *enters right.)*

JOHN: Work, boy, get to work!

*(*JOHN *exits left.)*

SAMUEL: My father treats his employees better than this. I've messed up my life so badly that I'm not worthy to be his son any more. But maybe if I go home and ask him to hire me as a farmhand, he will. At least I won't starve working for Dad.

(SAMUEL *exits right.*)

Act 4

(JONATHAN *waits outside his house at stage left, his hand shielding his eyes from the sun.* JESSE *enters left.*)

JESSE: How long are you going to stand there waiting for Samuel to come back home? You know he never will.

JONATHAN: Maybe not. But I have a feeling he needs me.

JESSE: All he ever wanted was your money.

JONATHAN: Maybe you're right. But he's still my son, and I love him.

JESSE: Come on inside, Dad.

JONATHAN: Wait! I see something.

JESSE: Where?

JONATHAN: There. *(He points to stage right.)*

(SAMUEL *enters from right. His head is down, and he looks discouraged.*)

JONATHAN: It's Samuel! (JONATHAN *runs to him.*) Welcome home, Son.

SAMUEL: Father, I have sinned against God and against you. I'm not worthy to be called your son. But I'm so hungry. Would you give me a job as a hired hand?

JONATHAN: Jesse, tell the cook to fix a feast for us tonight. We're going to celebrate Samuel's homecoming.

JESSE: But, father . . .

JONATHAN: Hurry. Tell him now.

(JESSE *exits left, very angry.*)

JONATHAN: Come, Son, you need a bath and some new clothes.

SAMUEL: I don't understand. Why are you treating me so well after the way I acted?

JONATHAN: Because I love you. No matter how you behaved, you're still my son.

SAMUEL: Thanks, Dad.

(They hug each other, then exit stage left.)

Act 5

(JONATHAN *and* JESSE *enter from left.)*

JESSE: I don't care what you say. I won't go to Samuel's homecoming party tonight.

JONATHAN: Why not?

JESSE: Because it isn't fair. I've stayed here helping you every day, but you never gave me a party. Now that lazy, good-for-nothing brother comes home after losing all the money you gave him, and you roll out the red carpet for him.

JONATHAN: Son, you're my righthand man. I can't tell you how much you mean to me. I guess I've been wrong not to thank you for being so faithful.

JESSE: A compliment now and then would help.

JONATHAN: Everything I own is yours. None of this will be Samuel's. He had to learn the hard way that he can't buy friends, respect, and happiness.

JESSE: Then why are you making such a fuss over him?

JONATHAN: Because your brother was willing to admit he was wrong and come home. That was a difficult thing for him to do.

JESSE: Sure, he knows where to get a free meal.

JONATHAN: No matter what he's done, I'll always love him. He's like a lost sheep who's been found. So many times I was afraid he'd gotten himself killed. When he came home today, all I could think about was celebrating his safe return.

JESSE: I think I deserve a party, too.

JONATHAN: You deserve more than that. Everything I have is yours. Can't you come to the party and celebrate your brother's change of heart?

JESSE: I'll try, but only because I know how much it means to you.

JONATHAN: Thanks, Son. It feels so good to have both my sons back home!

2 The Good Samaritan
Based on Luke 10:30-37

(Who is my neighbor?)

CHARACTERS

TOM
JIM
HITCHHIKER
TWO THIEVES
TAXI DRIVER
MINISTER
SUNDAY SCHOOL TEACHER
RECEPTIONIST
NURSE

PROPS

Briefcase
Suit jacket
Large wagon
Envelope

Act 1

(A street in a middle-sized city at 11:30 on a Saturday morning. HITCHHIKER stands center stage on the sidewalk, his thumb out as he tries to hitch a ride. He is nicely dressed in a business suit and carries a briefcase. TOM and JIM enter left.)

TOM: Look at that guy trying to hitch a ride in the middle of town.

JIM: I'll bet he waits there a long time. No one's going to pick him up. They'll think he's going to rob them.

TOM: What's a nicely dressed guy like that doing hitchhiking anyway? Doesn't it seem a little strange to you?

JIM: Maybe his car broke down, or he had a flat tire.

TOM: Whatever happened, I hope he gets a ride soon. This place is crawling with muggers.

JIM: How do you know?

TOM: My uncle's a policeman, and sometimes he has to cover this area on his beat.

JIM: Really? I didn't know your uncle was a policeman.

TOM: Yeah. He's always talking about people being mugged and robbed, especially around here.

JIM: Then let's get out of here.

TOM: Don't worry. It usually only happens at night.

JIM: Oh. It's only 11:30 in the morning, so I guess we don't have too much to worry about.

TOM: Hey, it's almost lunchtime. Let's go to my place. Mom will fix us a sandwich.

JIM: Your mom's home today?

TOM: Yeah. She's a teacher, so she doesn't work on Saturday.

JIM: Let's go, then. I'm super hungry.

(TOM and JIM exit left. HITCHHIKER remains on stage, his thumb still out as he waits for a ride.)

Act 2

(Time is ten minutes later. HITCHHIKER is still looking for a ride when TWO THIEVES approach him from behind, hit him on the head, and grab his briefcase. HITCHHIKER falls in a crumpled heap on the sidewalk. TWO THIEVES pull off his jacket, search his pants pockets for anything of worth, and leave with his briefcase and jacket. TOM and JIM enter left.)

TOM: Hey, what happened to the hitchhiker?

JIM: He's fallen down, and his briefcase and jacket are gone. Someone must have robbed him.

TOM: That's terrible. Do you think we should help him?

JIM: I guess we could call the police.

Tom: One of us needs to stay here and watch him to make sure no one else hurts him.

Jim: I'm not going anywhere by myself, not after what happened to that guy.

Tom: Then we'll have to stick together.

Jim: Let's both call the police.

Tom: OK. Wait. Here comes someone who might help.

(Minister *enters stage right.*)

Jim: I know him. He's a local minister. He spoke at our church one Sunday evening.

Tom: He's walking right toward the hitchhiker. I'm sure he'll help.

(Minister *walks along sidewalk, sees* Hitchhiker, *steps way out in the street to get around him, and walks on down the sidewalk as though trying to get away as quickly as possible.*)

Jim: Did you see that?

Tom: Yeah. He ignored him!

Jim: Let's go ask him to help. Maybe if we ask, he'll do something.

Tom: OK. But you ask him. You're the one who knows him.

Jim: I don't really know him, but I'll ask.

(Tom *and* Jim *run to catch up with* Minister, *who has walked almost to stage left.*)

Jim: Hey, Sir, please wait.

(Minister *turns around to face boys. He looks scared as though he thinks the boys are going to mug him.*)

Jim: Did you see that man lying on the sidewalk?

Minister: Yes, I did.

Tom: He needs help. Could you call the police and tell them to send help?

Minister: As soon as I can get to a phone, I will. I don't

know what good it will do, though. There are so many homeless people in this part of town.

JIM: He's not homeless. Somebody mugged him and stole his briefcase and jacket.

MINISTER: If that's the kind of neighborhood this is, I advise you to get out of it as soon as possible.

(MINISTER *exits stage left.*)

TOM: Do you think he really will call the police?

JIM: He said he would. But he may not do it right away.

TOM: What are we going to do? The hitchhiker needs help.

JIM: Here comes someone else. Maybe they'll help.

(SUNDAY SCHOOL TEACHER *enters stage right.*)

TOM: I know her! She teaches Sunday School at our church.

JIM: Good. I'm sure she'll help.

(TOM *and* JIM *approach* SUNDAY SCHOOL TEACHER, *who is walking toward stage left. As she reaches* HITCHHIKER, *she walks way around him to keep from getting too close.*)

TOM: Ma'am, can you help us?

(SUNDAY SCHOOL TEACHER *acts scared and starts to walk faster.*)

SUNDAY SCHOOL TEACHER: You boys ought to be ashamed of yourselves, mugging people at your age.

JIM: But we're not muggers.

SUNDAY SCHOOL TEACHER: Get away from me.

(SUNDAY SCHOOL TEACHER *hurriedly exits stage left.*)

TOM: She was really scared. All she could do was think about getting out of here.

JIM: I don't think we're going to get anyone to help.

TOM: They're all afraid they'll get mugged, too.

JIM: We've got to do something.

TOM: Here comes someone else.

JIM: Who is it this time?

TOM: *(peers toward stage right)* It looks like a taxi driver.

JIM: He'll never help. All taxi drivers care about is how big a tip they get.

(TAXI DRIVER *enters right. He could be pulling a large wagon to symbolize a car.* TAXI DRIVER *approaches* HITCHHIKER. TOM *and* JIM *watch him from stage left.)*

TAXI DRIVER: Oh, dear. Another mugging victim. He looks badly hurt. There aren't any pay phones near here, so I'll have to take this man someplace to get help. I think I can fit him in my taxi.

(TAXI DRIVER *tries to lift* HITCHHIKER *into his wagon. He has trouble doing it and is about to give up when he sees* TOM *and* JIM *watching him from across the street.)*

TAXI DRIVER: Hey, boys. Could you come over here and help me get this poor man into my car? I need to take him to the hospital.

TOM: Sure, we'll help. Come on, Jim.

(TOM *and* JIM *help* TAXI DRIVER *lift* HITCHHIKER *into his car. Then, together they all walk off stage left.)*

Act 3

(In a hospital emergency room. TAXI DRIVER, TOM *and* JIM *enter stage left as they help* HITCHHIKER *walk to the reception desk.)*

TAXI DRIVER: This man has been badly hurt. He needs help.

RECEPTIONIST: He looks pretty banged up, all right. You'll need to fill out some forms.

TAXI DRIVER: I don't know who this man is, so I can't tell you what his name is or anything else about him.

RECEPTIONIST: So you don't know if he has insurance?

TAXI DRIVER: No, I don't. But I'll pay for all his hospital

bills. You take care of him, and I'll be back in a few days to pay the bill.

RECEPTIONIST: But, Sir, this is highly irregular. How do I know you'll come back?

TAXI DRIVER: You don't, so I'll leave you some money right now. That should pay for at least part of his care.

(TAXI DRIVER *hands* RECEPTIONIST *an envelope.* RECEPTION-IST *takes envelope and looks into it.*)

RECEPTIONIST: My goodness, Sir, that is very generous. That should take care of all his expenses.

TAXI DRIVER: Good. Now, I must be on my way. Thank you, boys, for helping me.

TOM: You're welcome.

JIM: We were glad to help.

(TAXI DRIVER *exits stage left.* NURSE *leads* HITCHHIKER *off stage left to get medical help.*)

RECEPTIONIST: Who was the man who left all this money here?

TOM: I don't know.

JIM: Just a taxi driver, I guess.

RECEPTIONIST: Well, he certainly was generous. He doesn't know this man, but he left enough money to pay for his care for several days.

TOM: Wow.

RECEPTIONIST: Do you know anything about the victim?

JIM: No. He was trying to hitch a ride. Someone must have mugged him.

TOM: We tried to get some other people to help him, but they were too scared.

RECEPTIONIST: That taxi driver is certainly a good neighbor.

JIM: Yeah. He helps people he doesn't even know.

RECEPTIONIST: I guess when you think about it, everyone who needs help is our neighbor.

3 Ten Young Girls
Based on Matthew 25:1-13

(Be prepared for the Lord's coming)

CHARACTERS

ANN   GINGER

BETH   HELEN

CAROL   JANE

DARLA   MARY

EVELYN   MRS. DUNCAN

FAYE

PROPS

Bedrolls and flashlights for each girl

Act 1

(A parking lot in front of a church. MARY and JANE enter right.)

MARY: Are you ready for the camping trip?

JANE: Yeah.

MARY: I'm so excited. I've never been camping before.

JANE: It's no big deal.

MARY: I hope I've remembered everything.

JANE: What's to remember?

MARY: You know what our Sunday School teacher said. We're supposed to bring a bedroll, an extra set of batteries for our flashlights, some sunscreen lotion, and our Bibles. There was some other stuff, too.

JANE: Who cares what Mrs. Duncan says. We probably won't need half that stuff.

MARY: Aren't you even a little excited?

JANE: Nah. I've been on camping trips before. They're nothing special.

MARY: Oh. Well, I'm going to go to the store and buy some batteries for my flashlight right now. I don't want to be caught in the dark without a light.

JANE: You're worrying about nothing. The batteries you've got in your flashlight are brand new. You won't need extra ones.

MARY: Mrs. Duncan said we should bring extras.

JANE: What does she know?

MARY: Uh, well, got to go. Bye.

(MARY *exits right.*)

JANE: She's such a nerd. Anyone who worries about obeying every rule has got to be crazy.

(JANE *exits right.*)

Act 2

(In the church parking lot that evening. MARY, JANE, ANN, BETH, CAROL, DARLA, EVELYN, FAYE, GINGER, *and* HELEN *enter right, carrying bedrolls and flashlights. They all sit in a semicircle on the ground with their equipment in front of them.*

MARY: I'm so excited about this camping trip. I hope I remembered to bring everything.

ANN: Me, too.

BETH: I wanted to bring my puppy, but Mom wouldn't let me.

CAROL: Good! Puppies always chew on your legs and lick you. I'd hate to be wakened in the morning by a wet tongue.

DARLA: Same here!

EVELYN: When did Mrs. Duncan say she would be here?

FAYE: Soon, I think. I saw her loading things into her car when Mom drove me over here.

GINGER: I wish she'd hurry up. I want to get started!

HELEN: Me, too. This is my first time to go camping.

MARY: Mine, too.

HELEN: I hope I brought everything.

MARY: Mom checked everything off on my list as I packed. So I think I'm OK. I almost forgot to buy extra batteries for my flashlight, but I got them at the store today.

HELEN: I brought extras, too.

GINGER: So did I.

FAYE: Did I remember batteries? *(She peers into the center of her rolled-up sleeping bag, then puts her arm deep inside and feels around.)* Yep, they're in there. I can feel them.

DARLA: I brought extras, too.

EVELYN: Uh oh. I forgot extra batteries.

ANN: Same here.

BETH: Oh, dear, I didn't bring extras either.

CAROL: Neither did I.

JANE: I didn't either, but I'm not worried. It's not like we're going to be hiking around all night with our flashlights on. We'll only need them every now and then. I'm sure the batteries in my flashlight will last just fine.

BETH: If they don't, we can always borrow some from you.

HELEN: Sorry, I only brought enough extras for one change of batteries.

MARY: Me, too.

DARLA: Same here.

FAYE: I'd share if I had extras, but I don't.

GINGER: Sorry, I only have enough for my flashlight.

EVELYN: What are we going to do?

ANN: Don't get all excited. I'm sure we can figure out a solution.

BETH: I've got one. Steal their batteries!

CAROL: No, no. We'd get in big trouble, and Mrs. Duncan would send us right home.

JANE: Don't get so excited. It's no big deal. So we don't have extra batteries. We'll go buy some. The convenience store is only a block away.

EVELYN: Hey, that's a great idea. Come on, let's go.

MARY: But what if Mrs. Duncan comes while you're gone?

JANE: No sweat. She'll wait for us.

FAYE: Don't count on it. You know what she said about being on time.

GINGER: Yeah. She said if we weren't all here at 7:00 sharp, we would miss the camping trip and the pastor would have to take us home.

BETH: She was just kidding. I know she was. She wouldn't let us miss a great trip like this. I know she'll wait.

EVELYN: I think you're right. Let's get those extra batteries right now.

JANE: OK.

(EVELYN, ANN, BETH, CAROL, *and* JANE *exit right with their sleeping bags to buy extra batteries.*)

MARY: I hope Mrs. Duncan doesn't come before they get back.

GINGER: Me, too. I'd hate it if they got left.

(MRS. DUNCAN *enters left.*)

MRS. DUNCAN: Hi, girls.

MARY: Hi, Mrs. Duncan.

MRS. DUNCAN: Why are there only five of you? There are ten girls in our Sunday School class. Didn't they want to go?

MARY: Yes, but they forgot extra batteries.

HELEN: So they went to buy some.

MRS. DUNCAN: How unfortunate. Mr. Duncan has agreed to take us to the lake for our camp out in his van. It's parked across the street. But we have to leave right away or he'll be late for work.

MARY: But what about the other girls?

MRS. DUNCAN: I'm sorry they'll miss the camping trip. Remember, I told all of you to be on time.

GINGER: Well, let's go then.

MRS. DUNCAN: You get in the van while I tell the pastor to watch for the other girls.

(MARY, HELEN, GINGER, DARLA, FAYE, *and* MRS. DUNCAN *exit left.*)

Act 3

(In the church parking lot a few minutes later. EVELYN, ANN, CAROL, JANE, *and* BETH *enter right.)*

JANE: We got the batteries.

ANN: Thank goodness.

CAROL: Hey, where is everybody?

JANE: They were here a few minutes ago. Where could they have gone?

BETH: Maybe Mrs. Duncan picked them up already.

JANE: She wouldn't do that.

ANN: I think she would. She told us we had to be on time.

EVELYN: You're right. What are we going to do?

CAROL: We can't just stand here in the church parking lot forever.

JANE: I see the pastor waving to us from his study. I'll find out what he wants. Maybe he can help us.

BETH: Good idea.

(JANE *exits left.*)

CAROL: I have this sinking feeling that we missed the trip.

ANN: So do I. And all because of a few batteries.

BETH: Well, it isn't fair.

CAROL: I feel like crying.

ANN: Me, too. I really wanted to go camping.

(JANE *enters left.*)

JANE: The pastor said he'd take us all home as soon as he finishes his telephone conversation.

EVELYN *(sadly)*: OK, I guess.

BETH: We should have been more prepared. Mrs. Duncan did tell us to be sure we packed everything.

JANE: Mary kept telling me I should get extra batteries. I just laughed at her. But she was right.

BETH: Yeah. We really goofed.

EVELYN: Next time, I won't wait until the last minute to get things done.

CAROL: You know, maybe Mrs. Duncan was trying to teach us something else, too.

JANE: What?

CAROL: Remember how she keeps talking about accepting Jesus as our Savior before we get any older because someday it may be too late?

JANE: Yeah. But that's just a scare tactic. I'm wise to that game.

CAROL: I don't know. Look at us. We thought we had it made. But we missed our ride, and we didn't get to go camping.

EVELYN: I'd sure hate to miss going to heaven.

BETH: Me, too.

JANE: I'll have to think about that one for awhile.

CAROL: I know this much. Next year, if Mrs. Duncan takes us camping, I'm going to be prepared.

BETH: Me, too.

JANE: Hey, the pastor's ready to take us home. Let's go.

(They exit right, carrying their camping equipment with them.)

4 The Talents
Based on Matthew 25:14-30

(Use the abilities you have.)

CHARACTERS

MR. HUMPHRIES, a wealthy man
JAMES, an accountant
JONATHAN
MICHAEL
STAN

PROPS

Desk
Chair
Ledger
Pencil

Bell
Three envelopes
Three lists

Act 1

(In a study. MR. HUMPHRIES stands by his desk near stage right. On the desk is an open ledger.)

MR. HUMPHRIES *(Taps the ledger with a pencil):* I'm going on a long trip, and I need someone to help me make money while I'm gone.

(MR. HUMPHRIES rings a bell on his desk. JAMES enters stage left and walks over to MR. HUMPHRIES.)

JAMES: You rang, sir?

MR. HUMPHRIES: Ah, yes, James. I'll be going on a long trip soon, and I have some money I want to invest while I'm gone. Where do you suggest I invest it to get the best interest?

JAMES: Well, Sir, if it were my money, I would stay away from the stock market. It's very unstable now. I'd invest in people.

MR. HUMPHRIES: People, you say?

JAMES: That's right. Find some people who you think would use the money to make more money for you.

MR. HUMPHRIES: I'm not sure I understand.

JAMES: You might find a carpenter who needs money to buy wood for furniture. Give him the money. He could build the furniture, sell it for more than you lent him, and give you back your investment with a profit. Or you could invest the money in an artist who needs supplies.

MR. HUMPHRIES: What a brilliant idea, James. I like it very much. And I know who will get the money.

JAMES: Would I be impolite to ask who, Sir?

MR. HUMPHRIES: Not at all. I'll leave it with my three employees. They have worked for me a long time, and I know they're all talented. I want to promote one of them, but I haven't decided who. I'll give the promotion who whoever can increase my money the most.

JAMES: That's a brilliant idea, Sir.

MR. HUMPHRIES: Send Jonathan, Michael, and Stan to my office immediately.

JAMES: Yes, Sir.

(JAMES *exits stage left. While he is gone,* MR. HUMPHRIES *pretends to write figures in his ledger. A few seconds after* JAMES *leaves,* JONATHAN, MICHAEL, *and* STAN *enter stage left.*)

JONATHAN: You wanted to see us, Sir?

MR. HUMPHRIES *(looks up from his desk):* There you are. I have a job for each of you. I'll be leaving on a long trip today, and I want to invest some of my money so it will make money for me while I'm gone.

MICHAEL: Very good, Sir. How can we help?

MR. HUMPHRIES: I'm going to invest the money in you.

STAN: In us?

MR. HUMPHRIES: Yes. Jonathan, I'm giving you $500. Use it wisely so that when I come back, you can return it to me with interest. *(He hands* JONATHAN *an envelope.)*

JONATHAN: Thank you, Sir. I'll do my best.

MR. HUMPHRIES: Michael, I'm giving you $200. See how much more money you can make with it. *(He hands* MICHAEL *an envelope.)*

MICHAEL: Thank you, Sir. I'll do my best.

MR. HUMPHRIES: Stan, I'm giving you $100. See if you can make this money grow. *(He hands* STAN *an envelope.)*

STAN: Uh, thank you, Sir. But I wish you wouldn't give this to me.

MR. HUMPHRIES: Why not?

STAN: Because I'm afraid I won't do as well as you think I should.

MR. HUMPHRIES: Nonsense. Do the best you can. I'll be happy with whatever you do as long as you really try.

STAN: Uh, I'll try, Sir.

MR. HUMPHRIES: Good for you. Where is James?

JONATHAN: He's waiting outside the door.

MR. HUMPHRIES: James, come in here.

(JAMES *enters stage left.)*

MR. HUMPHRIES: James, I want you to be a witness to what I've done. Then you can keep track of how my investments are doing.

JAMES: Yes, Sir.

MR. HUMPHRIES: I have given Jonathan $500, Michael $200, and Stan $100. They are to use that money to make more money. I don't care how they do it, so long as they are honest and make my money grow.

JAMES: I understand, Sir.

MR. HUMPHRIES: I must leave now, or I'll miss my plane.

JAMES: Very good, Sir.

(MR. HUMPHRIES *exits stage right.)*

STAN: What are we going to do? I can't stand having so much money. I'm afraid I'll spend it on something silly and have nothing left for Mr. Humphries.

JAMES: You're good at making jewelry, aren't you?

STAN: Yes, I like to do that in my spare time.

JAMES: Then why don't you buy some supplies, make some jewelry and sell it for more than the supplies cost? You can earn money for Mr. Humphries that way.

STAN: But what if I can't sell the jewelry? Then I would have spent his money and have nothing to show for it.

JAMES: Use your ability as a jeweler and a salesman.

STAN: But I'm no salesperson.

JAMES: Make such beautiful jewelry that people will want to buy it.

STAN: What if I can't convince anyone to buy it?

JAMES: Then hire someone to sell it for you. You'd have to make your jewelry more expensive to pay his salary, but I know you can do it. You make beautiful jewelry.

STAN: I don't know. I'll think about it. (STAN *exits left.*)

MICHAEL: Hearing you and Stan talk gave me an idea.

JAMES: What's that?

MICHAEL: I'd like to raise goats. I think I'll buy some goats, feed them, and sell their milk. When they have baby goats, I'll sell the kids. I think I could put Mr. Humphries' money to good use in that way. And I can butcher some goats for meat to save money on food.

JAMES: That's an excellent idea, Michael. Let me know how you get along.

MICHAEL: I will. (MICHAEL *exits left.*)

JAMES: Jonathan, what are you going to do with your money?

JONATHAN: I have several ideas.

JAMES: Good. Let's talk about them.

JONATHAN: First, I'd like to invest a little money in some book-binding material. I've noticed some of the books at the library are wearing out. I think the librarian would pay me to rebind them.

JAMES: Good idea.

JONATHAN: I have a pretty good voice, and I've always thought it would be fun to sing at weddings and other social events. But I've never tried because I don't have a tuxedo. You really have to look dressy for those events. So I'll use part of the money to buy a nice tuxedo. Then I'll offer to sing for a fee.

JAMES: Splendid.

JONATHAN: There's something else I've always wanted to do.

JAMES: What's that?

JONATHAN: Promise you won't laugh?

JAMES: Of course not.

JONATHAN: I've always wanted to dress up like a clown and entertain kids at their birthday parties.

JAMES: That's a wonderful idea.

JONATHAN: So I'll use part of the money to buy a clown costume and makeup. Then I'll do a few magic tricks and tell some jokes to entertain the kids.

JAMES: I know who your first customer will be.

JONATHAN: Who?

JAMES: Me. My daughter has a birthday in two weeks. She would love to have a clown at her birthday party.

JONATHAN: Great. I think I can be ready by then.

JAMES: You're going to be very busy with all these plans.

JONATHAN: Yes, but I think I can do it.

JAMES: I agree.

JONATHAN: Well, I'd better get busy. (JONATHAN *exits left*.)

JAMES: What wonderful plans! I'm worried about Stan, though. He doesn't seem to think he can do anything. But he has lots of ability. Sometimes I think he just doesn't want to spend the time it takes to develop his talents.

(JAMES *exits right*.)

Act 2

(One year later. MR. HUMPHRIES *enters right.* JONATHAN, MICHAEL, *and* STAN *enter left.)*

JONATHAN: Welcome home, Sir.

MR. HUMPHRIES: Thank you. I had a good trip, but I'm always glad to be home. *(He sits in a chair by the desk.)* Now, let's see how you've done with my money. Who's first?

JONATHAN: I've kept a list of all my expenses and earnings. I gave all the money to James for safekeeping.

MR. HUMPHRIES: Good. Let's see your list.

(JONATHAN hands him a list.)

MR. HUMPHRIES: Hmmm, hmmm, ah, yes. Well done, Jonathan. I see you spent money for book-binding material, for a tuxedo, and for a clown costume and makeup. Your expenses came to $200, leaving you with $300. But in one year, you have made a profit of $700. So you have a total of $1,000 for me. I gave you $500, and you have doubled my investment. That's excellent. I'm proud of you.

JONATHAN: Thank you, Sir.

MR. HUMPHRIES: Now, Michael. Let's see your list.

(MICHAEL hands him a list.)

MR. HUMPHRIES: Um hmm, yes, oh, I see. Very good, Michael. You invested all $200 of my money in goats and animal feed. But by selling goats, goat milk, and by butchering some goats for food, you earned $400. You doubled my money. Excellent. I'm very pleased.

MICHAEL: Thank you, Sir.

MR. HUMPHRIES: Now, Stan, let's see your list.

(STAN hesitantly shuffles forward and hands MR. HUMPHRIES a list.)

MR. HUMPHRIES: There's nothing on this list.

STAN: I know, Sir.

MR. HUMPHRIES: Why is that?

STAN: I knew you wanted us to use our abilities to make your money grow. But I was afraid I wouldn't do a good job. I was afraid I would spend all your money and have nothing left to show for it. So I locked it in my desk drawer to be sure it wouldn't get lost. When I heard you had returned, I gave the money back to James.

MR. HUMPHRIES: If I didn't think you could bring a good return on my money, I wouldn't have given it to you.

STAN: Well, uh. . . .

MR. HUMPHRIES: I know you have talents. But you didn't use them. You let your fear of failure make you lazy. There's nothing I dislike more than someone who is too afraid to try.

(MR. HUMPHRIES *rings the bell on his desk.* JAMES *enters stage left.*)

JAMES: You rang, Sir?

MR. HUMPHRIES: Do you have the money I gave to Stan?

JAMES: Yes, Sir. *(He pulls the envelope out of his pocket.)*

MR. HUMPHRIES: Give the money to Jonathan. Stan has proven that he's too scared to use the talents he has. I want the money to go to someone who will use his abilities even if it means a lot of hard work.

JAMES: Yes, Sir. *(He gives the envelope to* JONATHAN.)

MR. HUMPHRIES: Stan, you're fired. Gather up your personal belongings and leave. I don't want someone on my staff who won't use his abilities.

STAN: But, Mr. Humphries, I didn't lose your money.

MR. HUMPHRIES: You didn't lift a finger to add to my money. If nothing else, you could have put it in a bank and let it gain interest. But you didn't even consider that. Leave now. I don't want to see you around here again.

(STAN *walks with his head down as he exits stage left.*)

MR. HUMPHRIES: James, do you remember me saying that I wanted to promote someone but I didn't know who?

JAMES: Yes, Sir.

MR. HUMPHRIES: I'm so pleased with the way both Jonathan and Michael have performed that I'm going to promote them both. Jonathan will have the new job I've prepared, and Michael will move up to take his place.

JONATHAN: Thank you, Sir.

MICHAEL: That's wonderful Mr. Humphries.

MR. HUMPHRIES: Now, let's go to lunch. I want to thank you for the good job you did while I was away. *(All exit stage right.)*

5 The Lost Coin
Based on Luke 15:8-10

(Christ's Love for Sinners)

CHARACTERS

SALOME, the mother
GABRIEL, the son
SELWA, the daughter

PROPS

Table	Feather duster
Jewelry box	Straw broom
Headpiece with ten coins, one of which can be detached	Trunk
	Chair

Act 1

(In SALOME'S *living room. A table with a jewelry box is at right; a trunk sits at center back, a chair near it.* SELWA *enters left.)*

SALOME: Hurry, children. I don't want to be late to the wedding practice.
GABRIEL *(from off stage):* I'm hurrying as fast as I can.
SELWA *(from off stage):* I'm almost ready.
SALOME: Where did I put my headpiece?

*(*SELWA *enters left.)*

SELWA: Which one?
SALOME: The one with the ten coins.

*(*GABRIEL *enters left.)*

GABRIEL: Which one?

SALOME: You know—the one I wear on special occasions.

SELWA: I know the one. It's beautiful.

SALOME: What could I have done with it?

GABRIEL: Did you look on your dresser?

SALOME: Yes. It's not there.

SELWA: Did you look in your jewelry box?

SALOME: Yes. But I didn't check the special drawer in it.

GABRIEL: I sure hope it's there.

(SALOME *walks toward stage right to a table on which sits her jewelry box. She opens the drawer of the box.*)

SALOME: Here it is! Thank goodness. *(She holds up the head-piece that has one coin removed.)* But what is this? One of the coins is missing!

SELWA: Oh, no!

SALOME: This is terrible. All ten coins are special to me.

GABRIEL: What are you going to do?

SALOME: I'll have to go to the wedding without my head-piece. There's no time to look for the coin now.

SELWA: We'll help you look for it when we get home.

(SALOME, SELWA *and* GABRIEL *exit stage right.*)

Act 2

(*At* SALOME'S *house a few hours later.* SALOME, SELWA, *and* GABRIEL *enter right.*)

SELWA: I can't believe how concerned everyone was about your lost coin, Mother.

SALOME: They know how special each coin is to me.

GABRIEL: I'll look in the courtyard to see if it's there.

(GABRIEL *exits right.*)

SELWA: I'll dust. Maybe I'll find it that way.

(SELWA *uses a feather duster to dust everything in sight.*)

SALOME: And I'll sweep every corner. It's got to be here somewhere.

(SALOME *uses a straw broom to sweep.* GABRIEL *enters right.*)

GABRIEL: I couldn't find your coin in the courtyard.

SALOME: Help me move this heavy trunk, Gabriel.

GABRIEL: OK, but you're going to a lot of work for just one coin.

(GABRIEL *and* SALOME *grunt as they move the trunk away from the center back wall.*)

SALOME: It isn't just one coin, Gabriel. It's a special coin.

GABRIEL: They're all special to you.

SALOME: Yes, they are. Each one is different. My headpiece is not complete without all of them.

GABRIEL: Couldn't you replace the lost coin with a new one?

SALOME: No, no! Each coin has come to me through a special event. So each has a special meaning for me. A different coin wouldn't be the same.

SELWA: What's so special about the one you lost?

SALOME: I got it when Gabriel was born. It's been a special symbol to me ever since. When I touch that coin, I remember that Gabriel is being sheltered in the safety of God's mighty hand.

GABRIEL: Wow! I'm going to look harder for that coin. I like the idea of having God keep me safe.

SELWA: Which coin did you get when I was born?

(SALOME *picks up the headpiece with the missing coin and points to a coin.*)

SALOME: This one, Selwa. See how shiny it is?

(SELWA *comes close to look at the coin and touches it gently.*)

SELWA: Ooh, it is so shiny.

SALOME: It glows, just like the sunshine in your hair. It reminds me of how lucky I am to have you for a daughter.

SELWA: Thanks, Mother. Tell me about the other coins.

SALOME: This one I got when your father and I married.

SELWA: It's beautiful.

SALOME: I got this one on the day your grandmother died.

SELWA: I remember that. It was a real sad day.

SALOME: Yes, but this coin reminds me of what a fine person she was and of how much she loved me.

GABRIEL: Do you have one for grandfather?

SALOME: Yes. I got this one shortly after his death.

GABRIEL: It's got a real bold design on it.

SALOME: That's right. Because your grandfather was a bold man. He wasn't afraid to tackle any job if he thought it was the right thing to do. And he loved God so much he talked about Him to anyone who would listen.

SELWA: I miss hearing all the stories he used to tell about his experiences.

SALOME: When I look at this coin, all those stories come back to me. And I can see him the way he used to sit on the doorstep of our house, drinking tea, and entertaining his guests.

GABRIEL: What are the other coins for?

SALOME: This coin was given to me by my best friend just before she married and moved away. I miss her, but I have this coin to remind me that we always will be friends.

SELWA: Here's a coin with the face of a man who looks very wise and kind.

SALOME: Yes. This coin is very special. It reminds me of the day I met Jesus of Nazareth. He came to speak at our village, and I got to hear Him.

GABRIEL: Is He the one who made the priests at the synagogue so mad?

SALOME: Yes. I think they were jealous because everyone wanted to hear Jesus, not them.

SELWA: Did you get to talk to Jesus?

SALOME: Yes, I went to Him with a very sore arm. It was all bandaged. Jesus touched it, and the pain went away.

GABRIEL: I remember that. You came home, took off the bandages, and cleaned the whole house.

SELWA: I remember, too. You were singing as you cleaned.

SALOME: Cleaning isn't my favorite thing to do. But I was singing that day because I was so glad to use my arm again.

GABRIEL: And what is this coin for?

SALOME: This one reminds me of another dear friend. She died when I was still a child. I miss her, but this coin reminds me of how wonderful she was.

SELWA: What about these two coins?

SALOME: They each represent your dad's mother and father. They welcomed me into the family when I married their son, and they have always been kind to me.

GABRIEL: I see why this headpiece means so much to you.

SALOME: Some people wear their headpieces as a sign of how much money they have. But I wear mine to remember how many wonderful people have touched my life.

SELWA: I hope I have a headpiece like this some day.

GABRIEL: Come on, let's look real hard for that coin.

(All three begin searching the living room again.)

SALOME: It's got to be here somewhere.

(SALOME kneels on the floor to look under a chair.)

SALOME: Hey, I see something under here.

GABRIEL: Let me look.

(GABRIEL kneels on the floor to look under the chair. He reaches way under the chair and pulls out the coin.)

GABRIEL: Is this what you're looking for?

(SALOME takes the coin from Gabriel, dusts it off, and looks at it.)

SALOME: Yes! It's the missing coin.

SELWA: Great! Let's put it back on your headpiece right now.

(SALOME *attaches the missing coin to her headpiece, then puts it on, and wears it proudly as she walks across the room modeling it.*)

SALOME: At last, all ten coins are back together. Thank you both for helping me find my lost coin.

SELWA: You're welcome.

GABRIEL: I'm glad we could help, especially since you got that coin when I was born.

SALOME: You know, I was wearing this headpiece when I went to hear Jesus speak.

SELWA: Was that when He healed your arm?

SALOME: Yes. He said something I didn't understand then. But now I think I know what He meant.

GABRIEL: What did He say?

SALOME: He said that people are like coins in the headpiece. When they come to Him, understand who He is, and accept Him, it feels like a lost coin has been found.

GABRIEL: Do you understand who Jesus is, Mother?

SALOME: I think I do.

SELWA: Who do you think He is?

SALOME: I think He is the one God sent to teach us about how much God loves us. I think He is who He says He is—the Son of God.

GABRIEL: And what are we to Him?

SALOME: We are God's children when we accept Jesus as the One who guides our lives.

SELWA: Wow! When I get my headpiece, I want a coin to remind me of who Jesus is.

SALOME: That's a great idea. Now, come with me, children, while I tell everyone that I've found my coin. They will be happy for me.

(*All three exit right.*)

6 Laborers in the Vineyard
Based on Matthew 20:1-16

(teaching the self-righteous)

CHARACTERS
SAMUEL, the vineyard owner
JASON, the vineyard foreman
ADAM, a laborer
JAMES, a laborer
MARK, a laborer
ISHMAEL, a laborer
THOMAS, a laborer

PROPS
Five checks made out for $100 each
Something to look like a row of grapevines

Act 1

(Outside a store in town. ADAM and JAMES come out of the store, center back, and walk toward center front as they talk.)

JAMES: How are you, Adam? I haven't seen you in ages.
ADAM: Doing pretty well. I've been busy lately.
JAMES: Doing what?
ADAM: Going to school.
JAMES: What are you studying?
ADAM: How to run a vineyard.
JAMES: No kidding.
ADAM: Last summer, I worked for Samuel Hawthorne, helping him harvest his grapes.
JAMES: You mean *the* Samuel Hawthorne? The one who owns the biggest vineyard in the country?

ADAM: That's right. He said he liked my work and that if I studied hard, he'd have a job for me in his vineyard.

JAMES: Wow. You'll be set for life.

ADAM: I hope so. I've been hitting the books real hard, because I don't want to miss this opportunity.

JAMES: Good luck.

(JAMES *exits left*. SAMUEL *enters right*.)

SAMUEL: Hello, Adam.

ADAM: Hi, Mr. Hawthorne. How are you?

SAMUEL: Fine, fine. Been studying hard?

ADAM: All year. I've been taking lots of agriculture courses.

SAMUEL: Glad to hear it. I'm looking for some extra workers to help bring in a crop today. Would you be interested? I'll pay you $100 for the day.

ADAM: Sounds good.

SAMUEL: Go on to the vineyard, and my foreman, Jason, will tell you what to do.

ADAM: Thanks.

(ADAM *exits right*. SAMUEL *exits center back*.)

Act 2

(In front of the same store three hours later. JAMES enters left. SAMUEL enters center back as though coming out of the store.)

SAMUEL: Hi, there. Interested in a job?

JAMES: Doing what?

SAMUEL: Working in my vineyard. I've got a crop that must be harvested today.

JAMES: Sounds good to me.

SAMUEL: Fine. I'll pay you a fair wage. Do you know where my vineyard is?

JAMES: Yes, sir. Everyone knows where the Hawthorne vineyard is. It's the biggest and best in the whole country.

SAMUEL: Ask for my foreman, Jason. He'll tell you what to do.

JAMES: OK. Thanks, Mr. Hawthorne. (JAMES *exits right,* SAMUEL *exits center back.*)

Act 3

(Three hours later, in front of the same store. MARK *enters left,* SAMUEL *enters center back.)*

SAMUEL: Need a job?

MARK: Yeah.

SAMUEL: How about working in my vineyard the rest of the day? I need some extra laborers.

MARK: Sure. Anything beats standing around doing nothing.

SAMUEL: Fine. I'll pay you a fair wage. Go to the vineyard and ask for Jason. He'll tell you what to do.

MARK: I'm on my way.

(MARK *exits right,* SAMUEL *exits center back.*)

Act 4

(In front of the same store three hours later. ISHMAEL *enters left,* SAMUEL *enters center back.)*

SAMUEL: You look like you've got nothing to do. Need a job?

ISHMAEL: I sure do. I was beginning to give up hope that anyone would hire me today.

SAMUEL: There's still work to be done. I'll pay you what's fair. Go to the vineyard and ask for Jason. Do what he tells you.

ISHMAEL: OK.

(ISHMAEL *exits right.* SAMUEL *exits center back.*)

Act 5

(In front of the same store two hours later. THOMAS *enters left,* SAMUEL *enters center back.* THOMAS *stands scuffing his shoes on the floor, looking discouraged.)*

SAMUEL: Need a job?

THOMAS: Now? The day's almost over.

SAMUEL: There's only an hour of work left, but I still need laborers in my vineyard. I've got a job for you for the rest of the day if you're interested.

THOMAS: You'd hire me for just an hour's work?

SAMUEL: Yes, and I'll pay you what's fair.

THOMAS: Sounds terrific.

SAMUEL: Fine. Go to the vineyard and ask Jason to put you to work.

THOMAS: Thank you, Sir!

(THOMAS *and* SAMUEL *exit right.)*

Act 6

(Immediately afterwards in the vineyard. ADAM, JAMES, MARK, *and* ISHMAEL *all work among some grapevines picking grapes.* THOMAS *enters right and joins them.)*

THOMAS: Jason sent me over here to help you guys.

ADAM: Good. We could use an extra pair of hands.

THOMAS: You all look tired. Have you been working all day?

ADAM: I've worked eleven hours so far.

JAMES: I got here eight hours ago.

MARK: I've been here five hours.

ISHMAEL: I've been here two hours.

THOMAS: I can't believe my luck. I really need the money, and all of a sudden I get this job at the end of the day. It's almost too good to be true.

ADAM: Mr. Hawthorne's a good boss.

JAMES: And this vineyard is the best place there is to work.

MARK: There isn't a better vineyard anywhere.

ISHMAEL: There's something real nice about the working conditions. Everything is so peaceful.

ADAM: It's hard work, but I always feel real good about being here.

MARK: I don't know what it is about this place, but there's nowhere else I'd rather be.

ISHMAEL: Something about it makes you happy even when you're tired and things aren't going as well as you wish they were.

THOMAS: Yes, there's something really special about this place.

(JASON *enters right.*)

JASON: Quitting time, boys. Line up, and Samuel will give you your pay. (JASON *exits right.*)

ADAM: Whew, what a day. I'm bushed.

JAMES: Come on, fellas. Let's get our money!

(ADAM, JAMES, MARK, ISHMAEL, *and* THOMAS *walk in front of the grapevines and move slightly toward the right, forming a line with* ADAM *first and farthest to the right, then* JAMES, MARK, *and* ISHMAEL, *with* THOMAS *last and farthest left.*)

ADAM: I'm not sure where we're supposed to stand, but Jason went this way. So I guess this is the right place.

(SAMUEL *enters left. In his hand are five checks. He approaches* THOMAS *first.*)

SAMUEL: Thanks for your help, Thomas. Here's a $100 check.

THOMAS: Wow, thanks a lot.

SAMUEL: Ishmael, here's your $100 check. Thanks for your work.

ADAM (*whispers to* JAMES): If they're getting $100, we ought to get a bunch more because we worked a lot longer.

JAMES: I could use the extra cash.

SAMUEL: Mark, thanks for your help. Here's a $100 check.

MARK: Thank you.

SAMUEL: James, you worked hard, and I appreciate it. Here's $100.

JAMES (*Looks disappointed*): Uh, well, uh, thanks.

SAMUEL: Adam, I'm proud of the work you did. You stuck with it all day. Here's your $100 check.

ADAM: $100?

SAMUEL: Yes. That's what you agreed to work for.

ADAM: But I worked all day, longer than the others, and you gave them the same wage. I thought you'd pay me more.

SAMUEL: I haven't cheated you. I paid you what I agreed to pay you. I chose to pay James, Mark, Ishmael, and Thomas the same thing. It's my vineyard and my money, and it pleases me to reward you equally.

ADAM: What a rip-off!

JAMES: You said you'd pay me what was fair. Do you think it's fair to pay me the same thing that Thomas got, even though I worked nine hours and he only worked one?

SAMUEL: Did you enjoy working in the vineyard?

JAMES: Yes.

SAMUEL: How about you, Adam?

ADAM: Yes. Things are really nice here.

SAMUEL: Mark?

MARK: Yes, it was a good experience.

ISHMAEL: I enjoyed it, too.

THOMAS: So did I.

ADAM: Of course, you did. You just worked one hour, and look how much money you got.

SAMUEL: Don't ruin your good experience here by getting jealous. I pay everyone equally. But only the people who stay here all day benefit from the surroundings the whole day. Thomas got the same reward you got, but for most of the day he didn't get to be in this place.

ISHMAEL: That's true. I wish I had been here all day instead of just three hours. I was feeling pretty rotten before Mr. Hawthorne hired me. Nothing seemed to go right, and everyone around me was in a rotten mood.

MARK: These last six hours have been pretty neat.

JAMES: I have to admit the nine hours I worked here have been some of the best hours of my life.

ADAM: You all have a point. I got so wrapped up in the money I thought I would make that I forgot what a great place this is. It makes me want to stay forever.

SAMUEL: I'm glad you are beginning to understand.

JAMES: It's not an easy thing to understand. We're so used to thinking about money as the measure of how well we do that we forget about anything else.

ADAM: I guess you should all be jealous of me, because I've been in this super place all day.

THOMAS: We're not jealous. We're just glad for you.

ADAM: And I guess I'm glad for you, too, even though I did feel upset at first.

SAMUEL: It's closing time. I'll need more workers tomorrow, so if you're satisfied with the way I pay, come back first thing in the morning, and there will be jobs waiting for you.

(ADAM, JAMES, MARK, ISHMAEL, *and* THOMAS *ad lib various ways of telling* SAMUEL *thanks and good night. Then they exit, leaving* SAMUEL *alone on stage.*)

SAMUEL: I asked a lot of people to work for me, but not many are willing to do it on my terms. I'm glad these people could accept my way of doing things. They're good workers, and I want them in my vineyard.

7 The Unmerciful Servant
Based on Matthew 18:23-35

(law of forgiveness)

CHARACTERS

KING SETH
JARED, a servant
ENOCH, a servant
JOSHUA, a jailer
AHAB, a servant
HOSEA, a servant

PROPS

One table
Three chairs
Large chair to look like throne

Act 1

(In the servants' quarters. JARED, AHAB, *and* HOSEA *sit at a table near left front.)*

AHAB: Did you hear about King Seth's latest decree?
HOSEA: No.
JARED: What's he done this time?
AHAB: He's calling in all his debts.
HOSEA: You mean everyone who owes him money will have to pay up?
AHAB: That's right.
JARED *(agitated):* Why is he doing that?
AHAB: He's tired of people borrowing money and never paying it back.

HOSEA: He's got so much money, he'd never miss a few dollars.

AHAB: I'm glad I don't owe him anything.

HOSEA: I owe him $100. I borrowed it to help pay medical bills when my wife had our baby. I think I can pay it all back if he gives me a couple of months.

AHAB: You're looking awfully pale, Jared. Do you owe King Seth money?

JARED: Uh, yeah.

HOSEA: You do?

AHAB: How much?

JARED: More than I can ever repay.

HOSEA: How much is that?

JARED: $100,000.

AHAB: What!?

HOSEA: How did you ever work up such a big debt?

JARED: It was one thing after another. Our house burned down. King Seth lent me money to build a new one. Then my son hurt himself in an accident and we had lots of doctor bills. I didn't want to ask the king for more money, so I started gambling. I thought I could win enough to pay the doctor. But I lost all my money and owed gambling debts I couldn't pay.

AHAB: You should have asked us for help.

HOSEA: Yeah. We don't have much money, but we could have helped a little.

JARED: I didn't want to bother you. And I was also ashamed of the gambling debts.

AHAB: You really had troubles.

HOSEA: I had no idea.

JARED: I finally worked up the courage to ask King Seth for help. He took care of my gambling debts and paid the doctor for my son's care.

HOSEA: That's fantastic.

JARED: He also paid for a specialist to treat my son.

HOSEA: King Seth is a special person.

JARED: He was a soft touch. I can't understand why he's such a successful king. Generosity is a weakness, and kings can't afford to be weak.

AHAB: King Seth isn't weak.

JARED: Then he's stupid.

HOSEA: What?

JARED: Not stupid. Crafty. King Seth knows that if he doesn't share a little of his millions, his subjects might revolt.

AHAB: I think he enjoys being generous.

HOSEA: Since he was so nice to you before, I'm sure he'll be nice now. That is, unless he hears you call him stupid and crafty.

JARED: I don't know. I've owed him $100,000 for three years. I've barely made a dent in my debt.

HOSEA: If you're making an effort, you should be all right.

JARED: That's the problem.

AHAB: What problem?

JARED: I haven't been paying him back.

HOSEA: You haven't paid him anything?

JARED: Well, I did give him $15.

AHAB: Only $15 in three years?

JARED: Yeah.

HOSEA: That's not so good.

JARED: King Seth never asked me for the money, and after awhile I sort of forgot about the debt.

HOSEA: You'd better start thinking about it.

AHAB: Yeah, because King Seth is throwing people in jail if they haven't tried to pay their debts.

JARED: I'm grateful to King Seth, but sometimes he acts so high and mighty. Here he is, a rich king, but look how he treats people who can't pay him back.

HOSEA: He thinks people take advantage of him.

AHAB: You've got to admit, Jared. It sounds like that's what you're doing.

JARED: How can I get back in the king's good graces?

AHAB: Start making a real effort to pay him back.

(ENOCH *enters right.*)

ENOCH: Jared, I've been looking everywhere for you.
JARED: Why?
ENOCH: King Seth wants to see you.
JARED: Oh, no.
AHAB: You'd better go and get it over with.
HOSEA: Yeah. Take your punishment like a man.
JARED: I'll say my good-byes now in case I'm thrown in jail.
HOSEA: Maybe it won't be as bad as you think.

(JARED *and* ENOCH *exit right.*)

HOSEA: I wonder if we'll ever see him again.
AHAB: With a debt that big, he'll spend the rest of his life in jail.

(AHAB *and* HOSEA *exit left.*)

Act 2

(*In throne room moments later.* KING SETH *sits on a throne at center stage.* JARED *enters right and keeps as much distance between himself and the king as possible.*)

JARED: You called for me, King Seth?
King Seth: Yes, I did. Come here.

(JARED *slowly shuffles toward the throne.*)

KING SETH: My accountant tells me you've never repaid the $100,000 I loaned you three years ago.
JARED (*miserably*): That's right, sir.
KING SETH: Why haven't you repaid me?
JARED: It would take a lifetime to pay a debt that large.
KING SETH: But you haven't even tried.
JARED: I did pay a little.
KING SETH: One payment of $15 is hardly trying.
JARED (*Mumbles*): Yes, your Majesty.

KING SETH: What do you have to say for yourself?

JARED: Uh, well, uh . . .

KING SETH: Jailer Joshua, come here!

(JOSHUA enters stage left. He stands beside and a little to the left of the throne and remains there until dismissed.)

KING SETH: Speak up, Jared, or I'll have you thrown in jail, your wife and children sold as slaves, and all your possessions auctioned off to pay the debt.

JARED: No, please, not that. *(Falls to his knees and begs.)* I couldn't bear to think of my family as slaves. Be patient with me. I'll find a way to pay you back.

KING SETH: For heaven's sake, get up off the floor, Jared. I can't stand to see a man beg.

(Instead of standing, JARED lies full length on the floor.)

JARED: I beg you, give me just a little more time.

KING SETH: Stand up!

(A frightened JARED stands.)

KING SETH: That's better. How much time do you need?

JARED: If I sell all my possessions, find another job in the evenings and borrow money from my relatives, maybe I can pay you back in five years.

KING SETH: I can't have you do that. I'll tell you what I'll do.

JARED: Anything, your Majesty. But please don't sell my family as slaves.

KING SETH: I'm going to forgive your debt.

JARED: You're what?

KING SETH: I'm going to wipe the slate clean. As of this moment, you don't owe me anything.

JARED: Your Majesty! How can I ever thank you?

KING SETH: You can thank me by forgiving others when they need to be forgiven.

JARED: I will, I will!

KING SETH: You may go, jailer. I won't be needing you.

(JOSHUA *exits left*.)

JARED: Everyone says you are a fair and honest king. You're also merciful. Thank you, thank you.

KING SETH: Quit talking and get back to work.

JARED: Yes, Sir. (JARED *turns toward right as if to go*.)

KING SETH: One more thing.

(JARED *turns back toward the king*.)

KING SETH: Pay your debts more promptly in the future. Another lender might not be as generous as I am.

JARED: Yes, Sir.

KING SETH: You may go now.

(JARED *quickly exits right*.)

Act 3

(In the servant's quarters moments later. AHAB *and* HOSEA *sit at the table near center left.* JARED *enters right.)*

HOSEA: You look pleased, Jared.

AHAB: Does this mean you're not going to jail?

JARED: You'll never believe this. King Seth forgave my entire debt!

AHAB: All $100,000?

JARED: That's right.

HOSEA: You're the luckiest person I ever met.

JARED: At first, he threatened to throw me in jail, sell my family as slaves, and auction off all I own to pay the debt.

AHAB: What changed his mind?

JARED: I pleaded with him, and he felt sorry for me.

HOSEA: The king has heart!

AHAB: He surely does.

(ENOCH *enters left*.)

HOSEA: Hi, Enoch.

ENOCH: Hello.

AHAB: How's it going?

ENOCH: OK. Here's the dollar I owe you, Ahab.

AHAB: Thanks.

ENOCH: And here's the two dollars I owe you, Hosea.

HOSEA: Thanks. I only loaned it to you a month ago.

ENOCH: I like to repay my debts as soon as I can.

JARED: Hey, you owe me $10. Remember?

ENOCH: I know, but I haven't got it right now. Can you wait until next month?

JARED: No. You paid Ahab and Hosea. I expect you to pay me, too.

ENOCH: I'll pay you next month, I promise. Things haven't been going too well lately. My wife's been ill.

JARED: Save it for the judge. Pay now, or I'll call the jailer and have you tossed in jail.

ENOCH: Please, not that. If I'm in jail, there will be no one to care for my wife.

JARED: You should have thought of that before. I've run out of patience with borrowers like you.

ENOCH: But I don't have $10.

JARED *(calls in a loud voice):* Joshua!

(JOSHUA *enters left.*)

JOSHUA: You called?

JARED: Enoch owes me money and refuses to repay me. Throw him in jail.

JOSHUA: As you wish.

(JOSHUA *grabs* ENOCH *by the arm and drags him offstage left while* ENOCH *cries for mercy.*)

JARED: That will teach him to pay his bills!

HOSEA: I can't believe you did that.

JARED: He paid both of you and deliberately left me out.

AHAB: How could you treat Enoch that way after what King Seth did for you?

JARED: King Seth is a pushover. Just because he's such a softie doesn't mean I have to be.

(JOSHUA *and* AHAB *exit left, shaking their heads.*)

JARED: Good riddance. Who needs them, anyway?

Act 4

(In the throne room. KING SETH *sits on his throne.* HOSEA *and* AHAB *stand to the right.)*

KING SETH: Jared did what?
HOSEA: He had Enoch thrown in jail because he couldn't pay the $10 he owed Jared.
KING SETH: You saw this too, Ahab?
AHAB: Yes, Your Majesty.
KING SETH: Thank you for telling me. You may go now.

(HOSEA *and* AHAB *exit right.*)

KING SETH: Joshua!

(JOSHUA *enters left.*)

JOSHUA: Yes, your Majesty?
KING SETH: Bring Jared to me.
JOSHUA: Right away, your Majesty.

(JOSHUA *exits left, then returns with* JARED. *He shoves* JARED *in the back to make him move forward.*)

JARED: Cut it out. You're hurting me.

(JOSHUA *prods* JARED *until he stands just left of the throne. Then* JOSHUA *exits left.*)

KING SETH: Stand up straight, Jared.
JARED: Uh, yes, Your Majesty.
KING SETH: Is it true that you had Enoch thrown in jail because he owes you $10?
JARED: Yeah, it's true.

KING SETH: I forgave you a $100,000 debt. Why didn't you show Enoch the same kind of compassion?

JARED: It was only $10, and I figured he could afford it.

KING SETH: I can't believe you're so ungrateful.

JARED: I thought he was holding out on me.

KING SETH: You're a disgrace. You told me you would forgive others as I forgave you. But you didn't live up to that promise. As of now, your debt is reinstated. You'll go to jail until you pay it all.

JARED: Uh, perhaps I was a little hasty. I'll forgive Enoch his $10 debt if you'll give me another chance. Please? (JARED *gets on his knees and begs.*)

KING SETH: Don't try that routine again, Jared. It won't work. You were forgiven a huge debt, then refused to forgive a small one. *(Calls loudly)* Joshua!

(JOSHUA *enters left.*)

KING SETH: Take this man to jail.

JOSHUA: Yes, Your Majesty.

KING SETH: Then arrange to have all his possessions sold to pay what he owes me.

JOSHUA: Right away, your Majesty.

(JOSHUA *grabs* JARED *by the arm and drags him offstage while* JARED *speaks angrily.*)

JARED: Everyone says you're such a merciful king. Well, I know better. One little mistake, and you send me to jail.

(When JARED *and* JOSHUA *are offstage,* KING SETH *shakes his head sadly.)*

KING SETH: How can one man be so unforgiving especially after he's been forgiven so much? Maybe some time spent in jail will cause him to understand why I'm so disappointed in him.

8 A Friend at Midnight
Based on Luke 11:5-8

(Persevere in prayer.)

CHARACTERS

ALVIN
TONY
MARTIN

PROPS

Three loaves of bread
Two tables
Two beds
Two chairs
Blanket

(The stage should be arranged so that the right three-fourths of it are ALVIN's house with a door entering the house at center back. The door to MARTIN's house should face stage left with enough space between the door and the left edge of the stage for a bed on which MARTIN sleeps and a table with three loaves.)

Play Takes Place in One Act

(In ALVIN's house at 11:30 p.m. ALVIN looks at a real or imaginary wristwatch, yawns, and stretches.)

ALVIN: Eleven thirty. No wonder I'm tired. It's way past my bedtime. Guess I'd better get some sleep.

(A knock is heard at door in center back stage.)

ALVIN: Who could that be at this late hour?

(ALVIN *goes to the door, peers through the peephole in its center, then gets very excited.*)

ALVIN: Why it's my old friend, Tony! I haven't seen him in years.

(ALVIN *opens the door, and* TONY *enters.*)

ALVIN: I'm so glad to see you!

(They shake hands enthusiastically.)

TONY: It's been so long, I wasn't sure you'd recognize me.

ALVIN: We've been friends since kindergarten. I'll never forget you.

TONY: I'm in town on a business trip, and all the motels are booked up. Could I sleep on your sofa?

ALVIN: You'll sleep on the bed in my guest room. I keep it ready for special people like you.

TONY: Great! I sure am tired.

ALVIN: Tell me a little about yourself. I haven't seen you since the eighth grade.

TONY: I'm selling office machines now, so I travel most of the time. How about you?

ALVIN: I work at the post office. It gets hectic around the holidays, but I like it.

TONY: You, a mail carrier. That's funny.

ALVIN: Why?

TONY: Remember in the third grade when we sent Molly that silly unsigned letter?

ALVIN: Yeah. It said someone in class had a big crush on her and wanted to take her out.

TONY: Remember how she asked all the kids, one by one, if they wrote the letter?

ALVIN: Yeah. You told her I wrote it.

TONY: And you told her I wrote it!

ALVIN: So we both took her out.

TONY: And now you're delivering letters for real. I wonder what ever happened to Molly.

ALVIN: She's an elementary school principal.

TONY: No kidding.

ALVIN: Yeah.

TONY: How about Benny?

ALVIN: The kid who never listened in class and was always falling down and hurting himself?

TONY: Yeah. He was always the shortest one in class, and he always caused the most trouble.

ALVIN: He's a swimming coach at the high school.

TONY: Benny coaches athletes?

ALVIN: Yes. He stopped being clumsy in the tenth grade. That's when he started winning all kinds of swimming trophies.

TONY: Wow. What about Henry, the straight-A whiz kid?

ALVIN: He just got out of medical school. He's working at a hospital on an Indian reservation.

TONY: He was the smartest kid I ever met.

ALVIN: One of the nicest ones, too. Remember how we all went to him if we had a skinned knee or a sore throat?

TONY: Yeah. We always felt better after we had a talk with Henry.

ALVIN: Well, let me show you where you'll sleep.

TONY: First, I'm awfully hungry. Do you have anything to eat?

ALVIN: I'm sorry, Tony, but I'm fresh out of food. I'm going to the grocery store tomorrow. If I had known you were coming, I would have stocked up on pizza.

TONY: That's OK.

ALVIN: No, it's not. I haven't seen you in years, and I don't want you to go hungry. Let me run across the street to Martin's house. He may have some extra bread.

TONY: Thanks, Alvin. I really am hungry.

ALVIN: I'll be right back.

(TONY *lies down on the guest bed near stage right. He goes to sleep.* ALVIN *walks toward stage left where the door to* MARTIN'S *house stands. On the other side of the door is a bed on which* MARTIN *is sleeping.* ALVIN *knocks on the door. When there is no answer, he knocks louder.* MARTIN *moves and stretches in bed.*)

MARTIN: Who's there?

ALVIN: It's me. Alvin.

MARTIN: Go away. I'm in bed, and I'm too sleepy to come to the door.

ALVIN: But it's important.

MARTIN: So is my sleep. It's midnight. Go home and come back tomorrow.

ALVIN: Please, Martin, you've got to help me. An old friend dropped by a few minutes ago. I don't have any food in the house, and he's really hungry.

MARTIN: Tell him to phone ahead next time. Then you'll be prepared.

ALVIN: I will, but he needs food now, and all the stores are closed.

MARTIN: That's because store owners keep sensible hours. They let their employees sleep at night. Get the hint?

ALVIN: It's an emergency.

MARTIN: So is my need for sleep. Now go home.

ALVIN: But, Martin, I need some bread.

MARTIN: Go home, before I call the police.

ALVIN: All right, all right.

(ALVIN *turns away from the door and takes a step or two toward stage right. Then he squares his shoulders and gets a determined look on his face.*)

ALVIN: I don't know why Martin's so cross and cranky tonight. But I need that bread, and I'm not going to give up.

(He walks back to the door and pounds on it. MARTIN *is still in bed. He groans.)*

MARTIN: Who is it?

ALVIN: It's me again.

MARTIN: You have one minute to leave before I call the police.

ALVIN: Please, Martin, I need help. Just give me some bread, and I won't bother you again. I promise.

MARTIN: Get lost!

ALVIN: Please, Martin. *(He bangs on the door again.)*

MARTIN: Cut out the racket, will you?

ALVIN: Give me some bread, and I'll stop bothering you.

MARTIN: I said I'm too tired. Now, go home.

ALVIN: I can't. I need the bread.

MARTIN: Get out of here!

*(*ALVIN *slowly walks away from the door. He starts to pace back and forth in front of it.)*

ALVIN: What am I going to do? Tony's hungry, and I want to give him something to eat. I can't let him go hungry. Martin has simply got to give me that bread.

*(*ALVIN *walks back to the door and bangs on it with both fists.)*

ALVIN: Martin, wake up.

*(*MARTIN *is snoring as he lies in bed. When he hears the banging, he sits up, startled.)*

MARTIN: Who is it?

ALVIN: Me.

MARTIN: I told you to quit bothering me!

ALVIN: But I need the bread. Please, Martin. I have nowhere else to turn.

MARTIN: Oh, all right, all right. I'll never get any sleep unless I give you some food.

ALVIN: Thanks a million!

MARTIN: How much do you need?

ALVIN: Tony's pretty hungry. Better give me three loaves.

MARTIN *(Mumbles under his breath):* Three loaves. What does he think my house is? A bakery?

(MARTIN *puts on his slippers, shuffles over to a table at stage left, and picks up three loaves of bread. He shuffles to the door, opens it, and shoves the bread into* ALVIN's *face.)*

MARTIN: Here's your bread. Now go home and leave me alone!

ALVIN: Thank you, thank you, thank you.

MARTIN: You're welcome, you're welcome, you're welcome. Go home so I can sleep!

ALVIN: OK. You're just the greatest, Martin. Thanks again.

MARTIN: Good riddance.

(MARTIN *shuffles back to bed and falls down exhausted.* ALVIN *carries the bread from* MARTIN's *door to a table near stage right.* TONY *awakens, sits up and rubs his eyes.)*

TONY: Hi. I must have dozed off.

ALVIN: I brought you some bread. Now we can eat.

TONY: Super! I'm so hungry, my stomach is making all kinds of noise.

ALVIN: *(Opens a loaf of bread and hands it to* TONY.) Here. Sorry I don't have anything to put on the bread.

(TONY *takes the bread. He and* ALVIN *sit on chairs at the table and begin to eat.)*

TONY: This tastes so good! I haven't had anything to eat since breakfast.

ALVIN: No wonder you're so hungry.

TONY: I hope you didn't have much trouble getting this bread.

ALVIN: Oh, just a little. I just had to convince a friend it was in his best interests to pay attention to me.

TONY: Some friends are easier to convince than others.

ALVIN: Yeah. Some friends love you enough that they help you whenever you need something. But a few help only if they think that's the one way they can get rid of you. Martin's kind of like that, especially when he's tired.

TONY: Well, tell him thanks a lot. This is the best bread I ever tasted.

ALVIN: Almost anything tastes good when you're hungry.

TONY: I'm glad I was able to find your house.

ALVIN: Me too. It's great to see you again.

TONY: There's nothing like old friends.

ALVIN: Stay tomorrow, too, if you'd like, and the next day, and the next.

TONY: Thanks, Alvin, but I've got to keep traveling. We'll have to keep in better touch after this.

ALVIN: Yes. If you call before you come next time, I can have two huge pizzas waiting for you.

TONY: That sounds great.

ALVIN: We'll talk some more in the morning.

TONY: OK. (TONY *stretches out on the guest bed.* ALVIN *pulls a blanket up over* TONY's *shoulders, then quietly tiptoes off stage left as he whispers.*) Good night, old friend.

9 The Great Supper
Based on Luke 14:16-24

(Always be ready to answer God's call.)

CHARACTERS

JASON, owner of house   MAN ON CRUTCHES
THOMAS, head cook   MAN WITH BANDAGED
                             HAND
ABIGAIL, a secretary   MAN WITH A LIMP
Several men and women who are dirty or handicapped

PROPS

Desk
Stacks of paper to resemble invitations
Brass bell
Several tables and chairs
Plates full of fake food or fruit

Act 1

(In dining room. JASON and THOMAS enter right.)

JASON: I love this house. There's such a feeling of peace about it. I always feel better when I'm here. I wish I could share this house with others so they could benefit from it, too.

THOMAS: How would you share it?

JASON: I'm not sure.

THOMAS: I have an idea. You could invite people for a tour of your home.

JASON: A tour is so impersonal. I want them to stay long enough to really sense how wonderful this place is.

THOMAS: In that case, how about inviting them for a meal?

JASON: That would be an awful lot of cooking for you.

THOMAS: I love to cook. The more the merrier.

JASON: Then let's do it. We'll invite lots of people.

THOMAS: How many?

JASON: This place is large. We'll invite everyone we can think of.

THOMAS: Now that sounds like a lot of work.

JASON: Abigail will handle the invitations. She's such a good secretary that she'll have no trouble doing that. You take care of the menu. And I'll deal with whatever else needs to be done.

THOMAS: Should this be a morning, noon, or evening meal?

JASON: Evening, I think. Then more people can come.

THOMAS: I'll start planning the menu now.

JASON: And I'll tell Abigail about the invitations.

(THOMAS *and* JASON *exit right.*)

Act 2

(ABIGAIL *sits at a desk at stage left front. Piles of paper are stacked in front of her.* JASON *enters stage right.*)

JASON: The big supper is tonight. How many guests have said they will come?

ABIGAIL: Well, we sent out 500 invitations.

JASON: I know, I know. How many of them are coming?

ABIGAIL: Well, uh . . .

JASON: Don't hem and haw around. Tell me.

ABIGAIL: None.

JASON: What?

ABIGAIL: That's right. No one is coming.

JASON: What do you mean, no one?

ABIGAIL: They've all told me they can't come.

JASON: Why not? We've planned this supper for weeks. It will be an unforgettable experience.

ABIGAIL: Here's a sample of their reasons. Horace says he just bought a farm and must go look at it.

JASON: Can't he do that some other time?

ABIGAIL: Apparently not.

JASON: Why won't the others come?

ABIGAIL: Jonathan says he just bought some cattle and must check the herd.

JASON: He wouldn't have to do that tonight.

ABIGAIL: He said to tell you he's sorry he must miss your supper.

JASON: What do the others say?

ABIGAIL: Nathan just got married and doesn't want to leave his new bride.

JASON: Sounds like a pretty weak excuse to me. He could bring her to the supper.

ABIGAIL: Perhaps he didn't think of that.

JASON: I can't believe no one is coming.

ABIGAIL: Maybe you picked a bad night.

JASON: Bad night nothing. They're just too busy to do something worthwhile.

ABIGAIL: Maybe they don't know what they're missing.

JASON: They know. It was described on each invitation. They just don't want to take the time to come.

ABIGAIL: You're probably right.

JASON: I know I'm right, and it makes me sad and angry. I have this beautiful home I want to share, but no one wants to take the time to learn what a beautiful place it is.

ABIGAIL: Shall I cancel the supper?

JASON: No, don't cancel it. I still want to share my home. If the people I invited won't come, I'll invite others.

ABIGAIL: Who?

JASON: I'll invite people I don't even know. Take some invitations, Abigail, and give them to people who live on the street and sit on park benches all day with nowhere else to go.

ABIGAIL: But many of them are lame, blind, or crippled. They're so poor they couldn't afford a decent set of clothes to wear to your supper.

JASON: It doesn't matter. I want people to enjoy this meal, no matter what kind of clothes they wear.

ABIGAIL: I'll get to work on the invitations right away.

JASON: Good. When you see these homeless people on the streets, in alleys, and sitting under bushes by the road, convince them that I really want them here.

ABIGAIL: I'll do my best.

(ABIGAIL *exits left. While she is gone,* JASON *paces the floor.*)

JASON: I can't believe all the people turned down my invitation. There is such a wonderful feeling of vitality and peace about this house. If people come here, I know they'll feel better. Why can't they see they're passing up the opportunity of a lifetime?

(ABIGAIL *reenters left.*)

JASON: Did you find some guests?

ABIGAIL: Lots of them. And there's still room in the dining room for more.

JASON: Then invite more people. Look everywhere, under cardboard boxes on the street, in shelters for the homeless, rescue missions, everywhere you can think of.

ABIGAIL: OK.

(ABIGAIL *exits left.*)

JASON: I can't understand this. I provide people with a wonderful experience, and they turn me down. Well, they had their chance to experience this place and decided not to. I'm having my supper tonight whether they come or not.

(JASON *exits right.*)

Act 3

(In dining room. A row of tables goes from stage left to stage right. Chairs are placed behind the tables so that people who sit in them will face the audience. JASON *stands at stage right to greet people as they come in.* ABIGAIL *enters left and walks across to stage right to talk with* JASON.)

ABIGAIL: There are lots of people waiting outside your door.

JASON: Invite them in.

ABIGAIL: They may take awhile to get in here. Some walk with crutches. Others need help to walk, and a few are very dirty.

JASON: It doesn't matter. They're welcome here as long as they said yes to our invitation.

ABIGAIL: Then I'll start sending them in.

JASON: I'm ready.

*(*ABIGAIL *exits stage left and immediately reenters with* MAN ON CRUTCHES.)*

ABIGAIL *(Points to* JASON): Go to that man, and he will show you where to sit.

MAN ON CRUTCHES: Thank you! This is a beautiful place, and I haven't had a decent meal in months.

*(*MAN ON CRUTCHES *walks to* JASON *and shakes his hand.* JASON *leads him to a chair.* ABIGAIL *directs* MAN WITH BANDAGED HAND *to* JASON.)*

JASON: What have you done to your hand?

MAN WITH BANDAGED HAND: Four fingers were cut off during an accident at work.

JASON: Where do you work?

MAN WITH BANDAGED HAND: Nowhere now. They fired me after the accident because they said I couldn't do the work any more.

JASON: You're welcome in my house. Sit next to the man who's already at the table.

MAN WITH BANDAGED HAND: Thank you, Sir. I could use a good meal.

(MAN WITH BANDAGED HAND *sits next to* MAN ON CRUTCHES. MAN WITH A LIMP *enters stage left, shakes* ABIGAIL'S *hand and walks slowly toward* JASON.)

MAN WITH A LIMP: Sorry I'm so slow.
JASON: Take your time. I want you to enjoy your evening in my house.
MAN WITH A LIMP: It's the most beautiful place I've ever seen. And it feels so peaceful in here.
JASON: That's why I want to share it with you and others.

(MAN WITH A LIMP *sits next to* MAN WITH BANDAGED HAND. *Several other street people enter stage left, shake hands with* ABIGAIL *and* JASON, *then find seats around the table. When they shake hands with* ABIGAIL *and* JASON, *each ad libs a greeting and a thanks for the invitation. When everyone is seated at the table, including* ABIGAIL *at left and* JASON *at right,* JASON *rings a brass bell to call for the cook.* THOMAS *enters right.*)

JASON: Thomas, please serve the food now.
THOMAS: Right away.

(THOMAS *exits right and immediately reenters with a plate for each person at the table. When everyone is served,* JASON *stands.*)

JASON: Before we eat, let's thank God for our food.

(All fold their hands and bow their heads.)

JASON: Dear God, You are our provider, and we thank You for this beautiful, peaceful house, this good food, and the chance to share it with these people. Amen.
ABIGAIL: Amen. Let's begin.

(Everyone at the table eats and ad libs about how good the

food is, how beautiful the dining room is, and how peaceful the place feels. After a few seconds, JASON *stands up.)*

JASON: Thank you all for coming. You have blessed my home by coming here to share this moment with me.

ABIGAIL: We're glad you all accepted the invitation.

JASON: Because you came, you have enjoyed the benefits of this place. It is a place that will grow on you. When you leave here tonight, remember the peacefulness you have experienced. It will help you get through tough moments in your life.

ABIGAIL: Draw from the memories you have of this place, and you will find strength when you need it.

JASON: Others were offered the chance to come here tonight, but they turned it down. You obeyed the call, and you are being blessed because of it.

(Play ends as all stand up on stage, join hands, and begin to sing, "There's a Sweet, Sweet Spirit in This Place." JASON motions to people in the audience, inviting them to sing the song as well.)

10 Lazarus, the Beggar
Based on Luke 16:20-31

(Believe God's Word today.)

CHARACTERS

LAZARUS, the beggar
ABRAHAM
FIRST MAN
SECOND MAN
ZADOK, the rich man
LEMUEL, Zadok's brother
ENOCH, Zadok's brother
AZOR, Zadok's brother
JACOB, Zadok's brother
MICAH, Zadok's brother

PROPS

Something to look like a gate.
White sheets to drape over the gate.
A few coins
A crust of dry bread
A pouch to be worn around LAZARUS's waist

Act 1

(Dressed in shabby clothes with one hand bound in a dirty white cloth, LAZARUS sits in front of the gate of ZADOK's house at center back. Five men enter stage right and walk by LAZARUS while he begs. The gate doubles as an exit.)

LAZARUS: Alms for the poor, alms for the poor.
LEMUEL: Quiet, beggar. *(He walks past LAZARUS and exits through the gate.)*

LAZARUS: Please, a little money for my poor family and my-self.

ENOCH: You don't fool me with that fake bandage. Why don't you do a good day's work like other men? (ENOCH *walks past* LAZARUS *and exits through the gate.)*

LAZARUS: Alms for the poor, alms for the poor.

AZOR: Here, you filthy beggar. Take this coin and clean your-self up, or your open sores will infect us all. (AZOR *throws a coin into* LAZARUS's *lap, then exits through the gate.)*

LAZARUS: Thank you, thank you. May God bless you. Alms for the poor, alms for the poor.

JACOB: You'll get nothing from me, you filthy beggar. I'm surprised my brother, Zadok, lets you sit at his gate every day. *(He exits through the gate.)*

LAZARUS: Please, a little pocket change so I can buy food for my family and myself.

MICAH: How about a piece of day-old bread, Beggar? *(He throws a piece of hard, crusty bread into* LAZARUS's *lap.)*

LAZARUS: Thank you. God bless you. (LAZARUS *breaks the bread in two pieces, puts most of it in a dirty pouch he wears around his waist, and hungrily eats the rest.)*

Act 2

(ZADOK *enters stage left front, followed by his five brothers.* LAZARUS *remains at center back by the gate. As the brothers talk, they slowly move across to stage right front.)*

ZADOK: I'm glad you came, brothers. We have a fine feast planned tonight.

JACOB: But what about that filthy beggar sitting by your gate? What will the guests think?

ZADOK: He's always there. Pay no attention to him.

LEMUEL: But he's filthy, and he stinks.

ZADOK: I'm doing my duty to the poor by letting him sit there. Besides, the dogs give him a bath every day by licking his sores.

MICAH: The dogs? Hey, that's pretty funny, Zadok.

JACOB: God doesn't expect us to put up with filthy beggars like him. Why don't you kick him out, Zadok?

ZADOK: He does no harm. And besides, he makes me look good. People think I'm very generous because I let Lazarus sit at my gate.

ENOCH: That beggar has an easy life. Nothing to do all day but sit and beg at your gates.

ZADOK: Like I said, I'm a generous man. *(Laughs.)*

AZOR: What will you serve at the banquet tonight, Zadok?

ZADOK: Stuffed lamb, tomatoes with rice filling, a delicious new dessert you've never tasted, and dozens of other tasty foods.

JACOB: I can hardly wait. You certainly know how to have a feast.

(ZADOK *and his brothers exit stage right.)*

Act 3

(LAZARUS *still begs at the gate at center back.* FIRST MAN *and* SECOND MAN *enter stage left and walk slowly across stage, talking to each other.)*

LAZARUS: Alms for the poor, alms for the poor.

FIRST MAN: Beggars should be outlawed. They're such a nuisance.

SECOND MAN: Leave him alone. He probably has problems we're not aware of. (SECOND MAN *throws a few coins in* LAZARUS's *lap.)*

LAZARUS: Thank you, kind. . . . *(He begins to cough uncontrollably, then falls over dead.)*

SECOND MAN: Poor soul. Looks like he is finally through begging.

FIRST MAN: Good riddance. One less beggar to bother us.

SECOND MAN: We'd better tell Zadok that his resident beggar is dead.

(FIRST MAN *and* SECOND MAN *exit through gate at center back.*)

Act 4

(ZADOK's *five brothers enter from center back.*)

LEMUEL: I can't believe our brother is dead.

ENOCH: Zadok was a fun-loving man.

AZOR: He knew the purpose of life—to live for pleasure and good times.

LEMUEL: He worshiped pleasure, and we must carry on the tradition.

JACOB: If he hadn't put up with that filthy beggar, he might have lived longer.

MICAH: Nonsense. It's been a year since that beggar died. He's not responsible for Zadok's death.

AZOR: Maybe not, but I was always afraid he'd give us some dreadful disease.

LEMUEL: Did you hear the doctor's report on Zadok?

ENOCH: Yes, he said Zadok died of a heart attack.

JACOB: I told him to quit eating so much.

MICAH: You know Zadok. He always liked food and planning big feasts.

LEMUEL: Poor Zadok. We'll miss his feasts. . . . And him, too, of course.

(The brothers exit stage right.)

Act 5

(ZADOK *enters stage right, crawling along in agony. He clutches his throat to indicate thirst. The gate at center back is now draped in white.* LAZARUS *stands in clean clothes in front of the gate, and* ABRAHAM *stands beside him.*)

ZADOK: I'm so thirsty. No one told me I would go to hell. I was a good man. I let that beggar sit at my gate, didn't I? Why am I being tormented? If only I had some water to drink. Won't anyone help me escape from this awful heat?

(ZADOK *slowly stands up, sees* ABRAHAM *and* LAZARUS *at center back and calls out to them.*)

ZADOK: Father Abraham, is that you?

ABRAHAM: Yes, it is I.

ZADOK: And is that Lazarus with you?

ABRAHAM: Yes, he is in heaven with me.

ZADOK: Have mercy, and send Lazarus to me with a cup of water.

ABRAHAM: I can't do that.

ZADOK: Why not? I let him sit at my gate during his lifetime. Now, can't he bring me a cup of water?

ABRAHAM: You lived a plush life, Zadok. You had everything. Letting Lazarus sit at your gate was nothing to you. You only wanted to make yourself look good, not because you wanted to help. Now, you're reaping your rewards. Lazarus, who has a good and kind heart, is reaping his.

ZADOK: Please, don't turn me away, Abraham. Send me water. I am so thirsty.

ABRAHAM: I can't do that. There is a great gulf between us. No one can pass from here into hell or from hell into heaven.

ZADOK: Then I'm doomed. But it's not too late for my brothers. Please, send Lazarus to tell my brothers that they must change their ways or they will go to hell too.

ABRAHAM: No, Zadok. Moses and the prophets already have told them about God and about how they should live their lives. If they won't listen to them, they sure won't hear Lazarus either.

ZADOK: But they know Lazarus died. They will believe if they see he has come back from the dead.

ABRAHAM: If Moses and the prophets cannot persuade them

to change their ways, then a man risen from the dead cannot persuade them either.

ZADOK: Woe is me, woe is me. *(He staggers off stage right.)*

ABRAHAM: Come, Lazarus. Let's talk to God for awhile. He wants to tell you how pleased He is with the life you lived on earth.

(ABRAHAM *and* LAZARUS *exit center back.*)

11 The Pharisee and Tax Collector Based on Luke 18:10-14

(humility)

CHARACTERS

HEZEKIAH, the Pharisee
MATTHEW, the tax collector
JACOB
RUTH, Matthew's wife

PROPS

Sack of money
Two chairs
Broom

Act 1

(On a city street. MATTHEW knocks on a door at center back stage. The door opens, JACOB enters and stands by the door.)

MATTHEW: I've come to collect your taxes.

JACOB: You again? Every time I turn around, you're wanting more money.

MATTHEW: I'm just trying to do my job.

JACOB: Anyone who would do your job ought to be ashamed.

MATTHEW: As soon as you pay your taxes, I'll be on my way.

JACOB: Here. (JACOB *pulls a sack of money from bag at his waist and thrusts it into* MATTHEW's *hands.*) I hope you're satisfied. I was going to use this money to buy food for my family. Now, get out of here.

MATTHEW: Thank you. I sure hate to keep food from people, but it's my job.

JACOB: Do it somewhere else. You've already done enough damage here.

MATTHEW *(Hangs his head):* I'm going. (MATTHEW *exits stage right.)*

(HEZEKIAH *enters stage left.* JACOB *remains standing in front of his door, looking sad.)*

HEZEKIAH: Good morning, Jacob. You look like you've lost your last friend.

JACOB: More like my last shekel. The tax collector, that poor excuse for a person, was here just now.

HEZEKIAH: People like him ought to be banished from the face of the earth.

JACOB: He took the money I was going to use to buy food for my family this week.

HEZEKIAH: Only a tax collector would be so thoughtless.

JACOB: What will I tell my children when they get hungry? I don't even have enough money to buy a loaf of bread.

HEZEKIAH: Remember how God loves a cheerful giver? If you drop even a tiny coin into the Temple money box tomorrow on the Sabbath, God will bless you.

JACOB: But I don't have even a tiny coin.

HEZEKIAH: Come now, everyone has at least one tiny coin.

JACOB: Not me. That awful tax collector took all my money.

HEZEKIAH: Then how will God bless you?

JACOB: I don't know. I try to live the best way I know how. Surely God understands that and will bless me even if I can't give Him an offering.

HEZEKIAH: Those mean tax collectors. They not only take your money, but they rob you of a chance to receive God's blessing.

JACOB: You mean if I have no money, God will not bless me?

HEZEKIAH: Probably, but only time will tell.

JACOB: I must pray that God will be kind.

HEZEKIAH: Yes, pray.

(HEZEKIAH *exits right,* JACOB *exits through door at center back.*)

Act 2

(*In the living room of* MATTHEW'S *house.* RUTH *is sweeping the floor at center stage when* MATTHEW *enters stage right. She looks up when* MATTHEW *enters, looking very sad.*)

RUTH: What's wrong, Matthew? You look sadder than usual.

MATTHEW: I don't know how long I can keep on collecting taxes.

RUTH: But it's your job. It's what puts food on our table.

MATTHEW: I know. But today the tax I collected from one man left him without food to feed his family.

RUTH: That's terrible. But you don't set the taxes. You just collect them.

MATTHEW: I know. But I feel terrible to be the cause of such pain.

RUTH: Think of it this way. You are an honest tax collector. If others had the job, they might force people to pay more than they owe. Then the burden on them would be even greater.

MATTHEW: I've told myself that a hundred times. But I still feel terrible when I must force people to pay taxes they can't afford.

RUTH: Stop thinking about it. Come to the kitchen and have some bread and fruit juice. You'll feel better when you've had a chance to rest.

MATTHEW: Maybe you're right.

(MATTHEW *and* RUTH *exit through center back door.*)

Act 3

(*In synagogue on the Sabbath. One chair is on each side of the stage near the front.* MATTHEW *enters stage right and kneels by one of the chairs.* HEZEKIAH *enters stage left and kneels by the other chair. After* HEZEKIAH *briefly kneels, he stands and confidently looks up toward the ceiling. Unseen by the two men,* JACOB *quietly enters through the door at center back and stands there.)*

HEZEKIAH: God, I'm sure you're glad to see me again. I'm happy to report that I've been a faithful follower of yours all week long. I've obeyed all your laws. I haven't stolen money from anyone, been cruel to them, or unkind to my wife. I fast twice a week, and I faithfully pay my tithes. I would never take the money people need for food as that awful tax collector over there did yesterday. Well, God, I've got to go, but I wanted to be faithful and pray to you today. After all, as a Pharisee and a leader of my people, I must set a good example for them.

(HEZEKIAH *exits left.* MATTHEW *remains kneeling. While still kneeling, he raises his head so his voice will carry to the audience, but he maintains a look of humility.)*

MATTHEW: God, I'm not sure if You even want to hear from me. I'm such a sinner. But I beg You, please be merciful and listen to me, for my heart is heavy. I have a job that forces me to take money from people who need it for other things. It hurts me whenever I must do this. Please help me, God. I need the job to feed my own family, and I am as honest as I know how to be. But I feel so terrible taking money from people who can't afford it. Please forgive me, God, and help me to live my life each day in a way that will honor You.

(MATTHEW *starts to exit stage right, but* JACOB *calls to him.)*

JACOB: Wait. Don't go.

MATTHEW: W-What? I didn't know anyone else was here.

JACOB: I was standing at the back of the synagogue and couldn't help overhearing your prayer. You're much too hard on yourself, you know.

MATTHEW: Aren't you the man I collected taxes from yesterday who had to pay me instead of buying food for his family?

JACOB: Yes, I'm the one.

MATTHEW: You're still speaking to me, even though I was so cruel to you?

JACOB: You weren't cruel. You were just doing your job.

MATTHEW: It's a thankless job. I wish I could give you money instead of taking it from you.

JACOB: Please, don't apologize. I'm the one who owes you an apology.

MATTHEW: No, no.

JACOB: Yes. You see, I hate to pay taxes, so I took out my anger on you when you have no control over the taxes. You only collect them.

MATTHEW: Most people think I'm responsible for all the tax laws.

JACOB: Well, you're not, and I know that. I was rude yesterday, and I apologize. You're a good man, I can tell.

MATTHEW: Thank you. You've helped me feel better.

JACOB: I'll tell you who I *am* upset with.

MATTHEW: The government?

JACOB: No, that Pharisee, Hezekiah.

MATTHEW: Why are you angry with him?

JACOB: Because he's so self-righteous. He tried to tell me that God wouldn't bless me if I didn't put money in the Temple offering box.

MATTHEW: Perhaps he doesn't understand how much God loves us all.

JACOB: He ought to. He's a religious leader.

MATTHEW: Sometimes leaders need a little help themselves.

JACOB: He needs to go back to Pharisee school and learn everything all over again.

MATTHEW: Let's just be glad God loves all people. Everyone needs forgiveness and understanding every now and then.

JACOB: I guess you're right. You're a good man, Matthew, even though you have an unpopular job.

MATTHEW: Thanks. I just happen to have a little extra cheese and bread at my house. Could I share some with you and your family?

JACOB: What a kind gesture! Thank you very much.

MATTHEW: Come along, then, and I'll get it for you.

(MATTHEW *and* JACOB *exit right.*)

12 The Sower
Based on Matthew 13:3-9; Mark 4:3-8; and Luke 8:5-8

(Spread God's Word.)

CHARACTERS

JACK
RHODA, his wife
TAMMY, a woman
HAROLD, a deputy
DONALD, a man
JESSICA, a high school student

PROPS

Straw broom
Sofa
Handful of tracts
Something to sound like a doorbell

Act 1

(In living room. JACK lies on the couch while RHODA uses a straw broom to sweep the floor near stage front left.)

JACK: I don't think I'll go anywhere today.

RHODA: Are you going to just lie around on that couch all day?

JACK: Well, things are slow in the construction business these days, so I'm going to take advantage of the free time. I think I'll take a nap.

(JACK curls up on the sofa and begins to snore. RHODA grabs her straw broom and playfully prods him in the back.)

RHODA: Get off of that sofa right now.
JACK: Hey, that's me you're hitting!
RHODA: Get up!
JACK: OK, OK.

(JACK *stands up and gets on the other side of the couch from* RHODA'S *menacing straw broom.*)

JACK: Now that I'm up, what am I supposed to do?
RHODA: Remember what you said in Sunday School last Sunday.
JACK: What did I say?
RHODA: Don't you remember?
JACK: Uh, sure. I just want to see if you do.
RHODA: You promised to spend the next month telling everyone the good news that Jesus is the Son of God.
JACK: I just got a little excited. The Sunday School teacher was so enthusiastic, he made me feel like I could conquer the world.
RHODA: You made a promise. Aren't you going to keep it.
JACK: How can I?
RHODA: You did pretty well yesterday on the street corner.
JACK: Hmph! That's what you think.
RHODA: I saw you walk to that corner light by the all-night grocery store. You stood on that wooden box you dragged out of the garage, waved your Bible around and preached a pretty impressive sermon.
JACK: You were the only one impressed by it.
RHODA: I saw several people standing around listening to you.
JACK: They were laughing at me.
RHODA: Maybe some of them were. But I'll bet some of them listened.
JACK: Not a chance. Half of them were drunk or high on something. I thought for a minute one of them was going to rob me.

RHODA: That must have been when you pulled your pockets inside out.

JACK: I had to show them I had nothing worth stealing.

RHODA: But what you have to give is free.

JACK: But no one wanted to hear about Jesus.

RHODA: Maybe they were all wayside listeners.

JACK: What do you mean, wayside listeners?

RHODA: You know, like the parable in the Bible.

JACK: I've never heard of a wayside parable.

RHODA: Yes, you have. You know the one about the sower.

JACK: Oh, yeah. He sowed seeds. Some fell by the wayside.

RHODA: That's right. The sower was like a preacher, like someone trying to spread the good news about Jesus. But the wayside listeners weren't ready to hear him. His words went in one ear and out the other.

JACK: I'm not going to stand on a wooden crate on a street corner again. That method doesn't work for me.

RHODA: It works for some people, but maybe it's not your style.

JACK: My style is to curl up on the sofa and sleep.

(RHODA *shakes the broom at him.*)

JACK: But I guess I'll do something else.

RHODA: Like what?

JACK: Like clean out the attic.

RHODA: I did that last week.

JACK: Oh. Then I'll mow the lawn.

RHODA: The neighbor did that two days ago.

JACK: Then I'll wash the car.

RHODA: We took it to a car wash yesterday.

JACK: Then I'll . . . I'll just sit down and watch TV.

(RHODA *shakes the broom at him.*)

RHODA: Jack, you made a promise, and I'd like to help you keep it.

JACK: Come on, give me a break.

RHODA: Think, Jack, think. What can you do to spread the good news?

JACK: I don't know.

RHODA: Yes, you do. You've probably got a great idea in that brain of yours.

JACK: I guess I could go down to the county jail and hold an evening service. Pete and John hold services every month for the prisoners. Maybe I can help.

RHODA: That's a great idea. Why not call Pete right now, and see if he'll invite you to go with him?

JACK: OK, OK, I'll call.

(JACK *exits stage right, and* RHODA *follows behind him to make sure he does what he says he's going to do.)*

Act 2

(In living room a week later. JACK *is lying on the sofa again.* RHODA *is sweeping the floor near stage left front with her straw broom.* JACK *snores loudly.)*

RHODA: Snoring again? I'll fix him.

(RHODA *advances toward* JACK *with her straw broom and pokes him in the back.* JACK *jumps up and hollers.)*

JACK: You woke me up.

RHODA: You're sleeping on the job.

JACK: What do you mean? It's my day off!

RHODA: Have you forgotten your promise?

JACK: What promise?

RHODA: To tell everyone the good news for the next month.

JACK: But that was two weeks ago.

RHODA: There are four weeks in a month.

JACK: OK, OK. What do you want me to do?

RHODA: Tell me how things went at the jail when you held the service there?

JACK: They went so bad that even Pete and John were discouraged.

RHODA: Oh, no. What happened?

JACK: A few months ago, three guys who had been attending jail services accepted Jesus as their Savior.

RHODA: That's wonderful. I don't see anything discouraging about that.

JACK: They got out of jail six weeks ago.

RHODA: Great!

JACK: They're back in jail now.

RHODA: That's not so great.

JACK: While they were out, they robbed a liquor store and stole a car.

RHODA: Oh, no!

JACK: Pete and John couldn't understand it. The three men really seemed serious about becoming Christians.

RHODA: They probably were.

JACK: Then why did they end up back in jail?

RHODA: The answer is right in that parable about the sower.

JACK: What are you talking about?

RHODA: Why they landed back in jail.

JACK: I don't remember anything in that parable about jail, robbing liquor stores, or stealing cars.

RHODA: No, but it tells about stony ground.

JACK: Stony ground! Do you know what you're talking about?

RHODA: The prisoners, of course.

JACK: Would you stop talking in riddles then?

RHODA: Those three prisoners are like stony ground.

JACK: They are?

RHODA: Yes. They didn't have any training to help them become strong Christians. They didn't have any topsoil that the new roots of their faith could grow in.

JACK: I still don't get it.

RHODA: Well, look at you and me. We've been to church hundreds of times. Our parents taught us lots of things about what it means to be a Christian. We know about how we're supposed to act and what we need to do to re-charge our spiritual batteries.

JACK: Oh, I get it. Those prisoners didn't have that back-ground.

RHODA: Right. Once they got out of jail, they didn't have any teacher to guide them. They probably didn't go to a church that could help them learn how to grow in their faith.

JACK: If they'd had someone to help them, they could have developed the topsoil they needed to hold the roots of their new faith.

RHODA: Right. But without that help, they withered away.

JACK: Was it our fault they robbed the liquor store and stole the car?

RHODA: No, but maybe the next time they get out of jail, you and Pete and John can put them in touch with people who can help them develop the topsoil they need.

JACK: Good idea. In the meantime, I'll take a nap.

RHODA: Your promise lasts two more weeks.

JACK: But I don't know what else to do.

RHODA: There's Ralph's Bar and Grill down the street.

JACK: What do you want me to do, go in there and preach? They'd throw me out.

RHODA: No. Stand on the sidewalk. When people walk out of the bar, hand them a tract with our address on it. If they read it and want to know more about Jesus, they can call you.

JACK: I guess I could do that.

RHODA: Here are some tracts.

(RHODA *hands* JACK *a handful of tracts and points to stage right.*)

JACK: You mean you want me to do it right now?

RHODA: Now's as good a time as any.

JACK: OK, OK, but I'll never make another promise in Sunday School again, at least not when you're around to hear what I say.

RHODA: Quit complaining, and go spread the good news.

JACK: OK, OK.

(JACK *exits stage right, and* RHODA *follows behind him.*)

Act 3

(In living room. JACK *is on the sofa again, snoring.* RHODA, *who's sweeping at stage front left, walks over and pokes him with her broom.)*

JACK: Ouch!

RHODA: Get off the sofa, Jack!

JACK: Leave me alone!

RHODA: Not a chance. You made a promise, and there is still one week to go.

JACK: But, Rhoda, I've preached on a street corner, held a service in jail, and handed out tracts at a bar. What else do you want me to do?

RHODA: I want you to keep your promise for the rest of the month, that's what.

(JACK *sits up on the sofa.*)

JACK: OK, OK. What do you have in mind?

RHODA: First, I want to hear how things went at the bar.

JACK: I handed everyone a tract. Some people took them, said thanks, and put them in their pockets. Some people grabbed them out of my hand, then threw them in the street. And some people called me bad names.

RHODA: But you survived.

JACK: I had only one tract left when the manager came out to talk to me.

RHODA: The manager?

JACK: Yes. He said he was getting complaints from his customers about someone handing out religious tracts.

RHODA: What did you do?

JACK: I only had one tract left, so I gave it to him and told him I'd go home right away.

RHODA: Good for you.

JACK: At first, I thought he was going to call the police and have me thrown in jail. But when I promised to go, he left me alone.

RHODA: It sounds like a lot of those tracts fell among thorns.

JACK: Thorns?

RHODA: Yes. You know, like Jesus talked about in the parable.

JACK: Thorns is a pretty good description. Some of them were pretty prickly.

RHODA: When you spread the good news among people who are surrounded by bad influences, it's hard for the good news to take hold.

JACK: Yeah, the thorns and weeds choke out the plants that grow up from the good seeds.

RHODA: That's right. But even if your tracts went to people who have a lot of thorns around them, you're still doing a good job of sowing.

JACK: I'd rather do a good job of sleeping. So let me rest for awhile.

RHODA: Not yet. There's still work to be done.

JACK: What do you have in mind now?

RHODA: The high school is looking for a speaker to talk about career opportunities.

JACK: Me? Talk to high school kids? You're crazy!

RHODA: I thought you could tell them about being a carpenter.

JACK: Well, I do know a lot about that.

RHODA: And maybe you could tell them a little bit about the carpentry job you did in Mexico last summer.

JACK: You mean when we helped to build that church for poor villagers?

RHODA: That's the one.

JACK: But you aren't supposed to talk about religion in schools.

RHODA: You wouldn't be. You'd just be telling students how you used your carpentry skills to help needy people.

JACK: I suppose I could do that.

(JACK and RHODA exits right.)

Act 4

(In living room. JACK is snoring on the sofa again, and RHODA sweeps with her broom.)

RHODA: He snores so loudly, he sounds like a train. I'll put an end to that!

(RHODA prods him with her broom. JACK wakes up with a start.)

JACK: Why can't you let me sleep?

RHODA: You're snoring so loudly, I'm afraid the neighbors will turn you in for noise pollution.

JACK: Come on, Rhoda. I've had a tough month. You've sent me out to spread the good news all over the place just because of a promise I made in Sunday School a month ago. The month is over now, and I've lived up to my promise. I deserve some rest.

RHODA: Relax, Jack. I don't have anyplace to send you today. I just want you to sleep quietly.

JACK: I can't help it if I snore.

(The doorbell rings.)

RHODA: See, I told you the neighbors would be upset about your snoring.

JACK: Don't jump to conclusions. It could be anyone.

(RHODA walks to stage right to answer the door, while JACK sits on the sofa. TAMMY enters right.)

TAMMY: Is Jack here?

RHODA: Yes. He's sitting right there on the sofa.

(TAMMY *walks over to* JACK *and sits down beside him on the sofa.*)

TAMMY: I hope you don't mind me barging in this way, Jack, but I just had to thank you for helping me.

JACK: But I don't even know you.

TAMMY: My name's Tammy. A month ago, you stood on a wooden box on a street corner outside an all-night grocery store and talked about Jesus.

JACK: Yes, I was there.

TAMMY: Well, I heard what you said, and it changed my life.

JACK: It did?

TAMMY: Yes. You see, I was so sad that night. I'd been taking drugs and stealing so I could get money to buy more drugs, and I was so stoned most of the time that I didn't even think about taking care of my little girl. She's only three, and a state social worker took her away from me the day I heard you talking on the street corner.

JACK: I'm really sorry.

TAMMY: I'm not.

RHODA: You're not?

TAMMY: No, you see when I heard Jack talk about how much Jesus loves me, I decided I had to learn more about this Jesus person. So I started going to church, and the people there helped me get off drugs. Now I'm clean, and I've got my little girl back. I just wanted to thank you for helping me get my life straightened out.

JACK: God did that. I didn't.

TAMMY: But you spread the good news, and that's what I needed.

(TAMMY *exits right.*)

JACK: Can you believe that?

RHODA: Your good news fell on good soil.

JACK: But we decided the street corner experience was a wayside experience.

RHODA: One of those seeds didn't fall on the wayside. It fell on the good soil in Tammy's heart.

(The doorbell rings again.)

JACK: I'll bet that's Tammy. She must have forgotten something.

(RHODA *walks to stage right to answer the door.* HAROLD *enters.)*

HAROLD: Hi. You don't know me, but I wanted to stop by and tell Jack how much he has helped me.

JACK: I helped you?

HAROLD: You helped me more than you can ever imagine.

RHODA: Sounds like more good soil.

HAROLD: What?

RHODA: Oh, nothing. I didn't mean to interrupt.

HAROLD: About three weeks ago, you and two other men preached at the county jail. Remember that?

JACK: Yes.

HAROLD: Well, I was there to hear you talk.

JACK: You were one of the prisoners?

HAROLD: No. I'm a deputy at the jail. I listened to you guys over the intercom, and something about the way you talked really got to me.

JACK: It did?

HAROLD: Yes. You talked real down-to-earth. It wasn't preachy, and I could relate to what you were saying. I've been having a pretty rough time at home. My wife and I weren't getting along very well at all. But when I got home that night, we prayed together and asked God to make our marriage better. Now we are happier than we've been in years.

JACK: That's wonderful. Thanks for sharing your good news with me.

HAROLD: You're welcome. Don't stop spreading your good news, because you help more people than you realize.
JACK: Thanks.

(HAROLD *exits right.*)

RHODA: You're a hit, Jack.
JACK: Not me. It's God. He's the one working in their lives.
RHODA: You're so good at this, I think your sofa days are over. Stony ground doesn't stop you.
JACK: My sofa days are not over! I'll never give up my naps.

(The doorbell rings again. RHODA *walks to stage right to answer it.* DONALD *enters.)*

DONALD: Is this where Jack lives?
JACK: Yes. I'm Jack.
DONALD: You're the man who changed my life.
JACK: I did?
DONALD: Do you remember about two weeks ago when you were handing out tracts outside Ralph's Bar and Grill?
JACK: Yes.
DONALD: Well, I got one of your tracts.
JACK: I'm sorry. I don't remember your face.
DONALD: You didn't actually hand me a tract.
JACK: I didn't?
DONALD: No. One of the people you gave a tract to threw it on the street. I saw the tract and picked it up.
JACK: I didn't notice anyone picking up tracts in the street.
DONALD: That's because the manager was talking to you when I found the tract.
JACK: Oh, yes. He threatened to call the police if I didn't quit bothering his customers.
DONALD: I'm here today because you were passing out tracts there.
JACK: You are?
DONALD: Yes. You see, I was very depressed. I had decided life wasn't worth living. I saw your tract on the street.

I don't know what made me pick it up, but inside was the good news about how much God loves me. It made me realize things weren't as bad as they seemed. I followed the steps in the tract that showed me how to ask Jesus into my heart. Your address was on the tract, so that's how I found you.

JACK: Thank you for telling me. It means a lot to know that God touched your life through me.

(DONALD *exits right.*)

RHODA: I don't think I'll ever have to move you off that sofa again. You sowed fruitful seeds even on thorny ground, and now you're hearing about the successful harvest.

JACK: It does make me want to get out and sow some more seeds. But I'll need a few naps to rebuild my energy. And I feel a nap coming on right now.

(JACK *starts to lie down on the sofa when the doorbell rings once more.* RHODA *answers it.* JESSICA *enters.*)

JESSICA: Is this where Jack lives?
RHODA: You've got the right place.

(JESSICA *walks toward* JACK *and vigorously shakes his hand.*)

JESSICA: You're a neat man, Jack. I just wanted to tell you that myself.
JACK: Well, uh, thanks. But I don't understand.
JESSICA: You spoke at our high school the other day.
JACK: Yes, I did.
JESSICA: You talked about being a carpenter and building a church for people in Mexico.
JACK: That's right.
JESSICA: Well, I've been a Christian for a long time, but I've been afraid to let anyone know it. When you got up in front of the whole school to talk about that church and

no one laughed at you, it gave me the courage to witness more.

RHODA: That's wonderful.

JESSICA: What's even more wonderful is that I just shared the good news about Jesus with a friend of mine, and she asked Him to come into her heart. I'm so excited.

JACK: I'm glad you told me about your experience. I didn't think high school kids would be interested in anything I had to say, but I guess I was wrong again.

JESSICA: You sure were. Thanks for everything.

(JESSICA *exits right.* JACK *walks vigorously toward stage right.*)

JACK: I think I'll get out my wooden box and go stand on a street corner for awhile.

RHODA: But what about your nap?

JACK: The sofa will be there when I get back. Right now, I've got some sharing to do.

RHODA: I'll go with you!

(JACK *and* RHODA *exit right.*)

13 The Two Sons
Based on Matthew 21:28-32

(obedience)

CHARACTERS

ALLEN
SCOTT
RANDY, a neighbor
JEFF, Allen and Scott's father
MAX, Allen and Scott's grandfather

PROPS

Basketball
Basketball hoop
Two $1 bills
Two cans of paint
Clipboard
Door
Counter on which a cash register sits, optional

Act 1

(ALLEN *and* SCOTT *are throwing baskets into a hoop attached to the garage of their house near stage right.*)

SCOTT: Do you think I can make five baskets in a row?
ALLEN: Not you.
SCOTT: Just watch.
ALLEN: No, you don't. That's just an excuse to hog the ball.
SCOTT: No, it isn't. When I've shot five times, you can try.
ALLEN: OK. But hurry up. You're so uncoordinated, you
    could take forever.
SCOTT: I'll try to hurry.

ALLEN: You're about as unathletic as a barn door.
SCOTT: You don't have to rub it in.
ALLEN: Just shoot the ball, OK?
SCOTT: OK, OK.

(SCOTT *takes one shot. Then* JEFF *enters from door at center back.*)

JEFF: Your grandfather needs help at the hardware store to-
    day. Can you both help him stock supplies?
SCOTT: Not me. I need to practice shooting baskets so I can
    get more coordinated.
ALLEN: I'll go, Dad. Just give me a few minutes.
JEFF: Thanks, Allen. I'd help myself, but I'm expecting a
    call from an insurance client.
ALLEN: No sweat. I'll take care of it.

(JEFF *exits through door at center back. When he's gone,* SCOTT *throws the basketball and misses.*)

ALLEN: OK, give me the ball, Scott. You missed.
SCOTT: Just one more try.
ALLEN: You said five shots in a row, and you missed.
SCOTT: OK, OK. Here's the ball.

(SCOTT *bounces the ball to* ALLEN. ALLEN *catches it, throws it at the basket and misses.* SCOTT *retrieves the ball and throws it to* ALLEN.)

SCOTT: Go ahead, take another try.
ALLEN: But it's your turn.
SCOTT: No. I'll never be as coordinated as you are. I'm going
    to the hardware store and help Grandpa.
ALLEN: Then I'll practice some more.

(SCOTT *exits center back.* ALLEN *begins shooting baskets. As he shoots,* RANDY *enters stage left.*)

RANDY: How about giving me a turn?
ALLEN: Sure, let me try one more time.

RANDY: I heard you and Scott talking about making five shots in a row. You've already shot more than five times. Let me have a try.

ALLEN: Just one more shot.

RANDY: You're hogging the ball. Give me a turn.

ALLEN: It's my ball.

RANDY: But you're always coming over to use my football. Don't you think you should share your basketball?

ALLEN: Oh, I guess so. Here. Take a turn.

(ALLEN *throws the ball to* RANDY. RANDY *catches it and begins to shoot baskets.*)

RANDY: Didn't you tell your dad you'd go to the hardware store and help your grandpa?

ALLEN: Scott went, so I'm not going to worry about it.

RANDY: But I heard your dad say both of you were supposed to go.

ALLEN: You were eavesdropping!

RANDY: I can't help it! My bedroom window is right next to your basketball hoop.

ALLEN: Can't you wear earplugs or something?

RANDY: Don't be ridiculous.

ALLEN: Just shoot the ball.

RANDY: Are you going to the hardware store?

ALLEN: Lay off, will you?

RANDY: Sorry. I just didn't want you to get in trouble.

ALLEN: Don't worry about me. I can take care of myself.

RANDY: I've had several turns. Here's the ball.

(RANDY *throws the ball to* ALLEN, *who begins to shoot baskets.*)

RANDY: Shooting five baskets in a row isn't easy.

ALLEN: I know. But I figure if I practice a lot, maybe I'll be a star some day.

RANDY: Fat chance.

ALLEN: Says you.

RANDY: So, are you going to the hardware store pretty soon?

ALLEN: I don't know. Maybe.

RANDY: Your grandpa has some shelves down there I'd like to buy for my model planes.

ALLEN: Those shelves are real easy to put up. You could do it yourself.

RANDY: I know. My dad says he'll give me $10 if I help him clean out the garage and workshop this weekend. I'll use that money to buy the shelves.

ALLEN: I wish I had that kind of money.

RANDY: Don't you get an allowance?

ALLEN: Yeah, but it's not very much.

RANDY: I figured your grandpa would pay you for helping out at the store.

ALLEN: He does, but I don't get there very often.

RANDY: If you went today, you could get some extra money. What would you do with it?

ALLEN: I don't know. Maybe I'd buy a big bag of candy.

RANDY: Well, see you later, Allen. I need to get home and do chores.

ALLEN: See you.

(RANDY *exits stage right.* ALLEN *throws baskets. Then he dribbles the ball off stage right.*)

Act 2

(*In hardware store the same day.* SCOTT *enters stage left carrying two cans of paint.* MAX *stands behind a counter at center stage back going over figures on a clipboard.*)

SCOTT: This is the last of the supplies that need to be stocked, Grandpa.

(SCOTT *sets the cans of paint in front of the counter where* MAX *is standing.*)

MAX: Thanks, Scott. You've worked hard. Here's $5 for your trouble.

(MAX *digs into his pocket and pulls out five one-dollar bills.*)

SCOTT: Wow! Thanks, Grandpa. I'm saving up to buy blade skates. This will help.

MAX: You're welcome. I wonder where Allen is. Your dad said he promised to come over and help stock supplies.

SCOTT: He probably got so busy playing basketball, he forgot. Anyway, the work's all done.

MAX: You're a good grandson.

SCOTT: I wasn't going to come over, you know. I told Dad I was too busy, but then I decided to come anyway.

MAX: The important thing is I can count on you. When things need to be done, I know you'll do what you're asked to do.

SCOTT: I'll try to help as often as I can, Grandpa. Thanks for the two dollars.

(SCOTT *exits stage left.* MAX *puts his clipboard away.*)

MAX: It's getting late. I guess I'll close shop.

(MAX *carries the two cans of paint to stage right front, then begins to walk toward stage left front. As he walks,* ALLEN *enters stage left, dribbling the basketball. He almost runs into* MAX.)

ALLEN: Oops! Hi, Grandpa. I almost didn't see you.

MAX: You're getting pretty good with that basketball.

ALLEN: I'm doing better. Did you get the help you needed today?

MAX: Yes. Scott did the stocking for me.

ALLEN: I was going to come over, but I got busy. Next time, I'll help you.

MAX: Have fun with your basketball.

ALLEN: I will.

(ALLEN *dribbles the ball off stage right, while* MAX *exits stage left.*)

Act 3

(Near the basketball hoop at SCOTT'S *and* ALLEN'S *house the next day.* MAX *enters stage left and knocks on the door at center stage back.* JEFF *answers the door.)*

JEFF: Hi, Dad.

MAX: Hi, Son. I came over to talk to you about Scott and Allen.

JEFF: Were they helpful at the store yesterday?

MAX: Scott was, but Allen didn't come until closing time.

JEFF: What? Allen told me he'd help you, but Scott was the one who said he couldn't.

MAX: Scott spent several hours stocking the shelves for me. He's a good worker.

JEFF: Yes, he is.

MAX: But I need someone I can depend on at the store.

JEFF: I wish I could help, but I'm swamped with my insurance business. It's really growing.

MAX: I understand. What I'd like to do is have Scott come over after school a couple of days a week and a couple of hours on Saturday to help out. Do you think he'd be interested?

JEFF: He'd jump at the chance. Hey, Scott, come outside for a minute.

*(*SCOTT *enters from door at center back.)*

SCOTT: Hi, Grandpa. What are you doing here?

MAX: I came to tell your dad what a great job you did helping me yesterday.

SCOTT: Thanks.

MAX: I need some help at the store on a part-time basis. Would you like to come after school a couple of days a week and a few hours on Saturday?

SCOTT: Sure. If it's all right with Dad.

JEFF: It's all right with me, son.

SCOTT: Then it's a deal. I could use the extra money.

(ALLEN *enters stage right, dribbling his basketball.*)

ALLEN: Hey, what's up?

SCOTT: Grandpa just offered me a part-time job at the store.

ALLEN: That's great. Do you have a job for me, too?

MAX: Not right now.

ALLEN: But I'm a good worker.

MAX: You dribble that basketball well, but I need someone I can depend on.

ALLEN: You can depend on me.

JEFF: Can he?

ALLEN: Sure, he can.

JEFF: When I asked you to go to the store yesterday to help him, you said you would. But you didn't.

ALLEN: I got busy playing basketball, that's all. It won't happen again.

MAX: Scott proved he's dependable, so he's the one I'm going to hire. If I ever need more help and you convince me that I can depend on you, I'll offer you a job too.

ALLEN: You mean Scott is getting this job because he showed up at the hardware store yesterday and I didn't?

MAX: That's right.

ALLEN: You're not fair, Grandpa!

MAX: I can't afford to let my business slump because of undependable employees. I hope you've learned a lesson from this experience.

ALLEN: I sure have. Never let my brother get ahead of me.

MAX: He chose to do what he was asked, that's all. When you get out into the working world, you'll need to prove you're a dependable person or you won't go very far. I want you to learn that lesson now before it's too late.

ALLEN: Who needs work, anyway? While Scott slaves in the store, I'll perfect my basketball skills and make millions as a pro basketball player.

SCOTT: Don't be mad, Allen. I didn't know this was going to

happen. All I did was help Grandpa when Dad asked me to.

ALLEN: You're nothing but a clumsy, weakling brother.

JEFF: That's enough, Allen. Go to your room.

ALLEN: Ah, Dad!

JEFF: No son of mine is going to talk like that.

ALLEN: Oh, all right, but I'm a better basketball player than Scott will ever be. So I think I'd be a better worker, too.

(ALLEN *exits stage center back, holding his basketball in one arm.*)

MAX: One of these days, Allen will learn how important it is to be obedient.

JEFF: I hope that time comes soon.

SCOTT: Me too. Now Allen's mad at me because I did what you asked.

JEFF: It's not your fault, Son. Allen said he'd help Grandpa. Then he didn't. He made that decision not to obey all by himself.

SCOTT: I guess you're right. But I don't want him to be mad at me.

MAX: If he really thinks it through, he won't be upset for long.

SCOTT: I hope not.

JEFF: In the meantime, I'm proud of you, Scott. You may not be the best basketball player in the world, but you're an obedient son, and I couldn't ask for anything better than that.

SCOTT: Thanks, Dad.

(SCOTT, JEFF, *and* MAX *exit center back.*)

14 The Wicked Vineyard Tenants

Based on Matthew 21:33-46; Mark 12:1-12; and Luke 20:9-19

(a warning about rejecting Christ)

CHARACTERS

REUBEN, the landowner
LAMECH, the head tenant
ENOCH, another tenant
ISAIAH, MICAH, AMOS, representatives of the landlord
JOSHUA, the landowner's son

PROPS

Two hoes
Vine loaded with grapes
Several grapevines
Straw basket

Act 1

(In vineyard. REUBEN *and* LAMECH *talk as they stand at center stage.)*

REUBEN: Now that you've been on a tour of my new vineyard, what do you think?

LAMECH: It's very impressive. It has a nice tall hedge around it to keep thieves and animals out and to let everyone know where your vineyard boundaries are.

REUBEN: It had better keep out those pesky sheep and goats who wander on the hillsides looking for things to eat.

LAMECH: I like your winepress. There's plenty of room for workers to stomp on the ripe grapes and for the juice to gather.

REUBEN: What do you think of my watchtower? Isn't it spectacular?

LAMECH: It's one of the nicest I've ever seen. The storeroom on the bottom floor has lots of space, the living quarters above it are roomy, and you can see the whole vineyard and hillside from the roof.

REUBEN: I wanted it to be comfortable for whoever lives here during the harvest.

LAMECH: That will be me and my helper, Enoch. We'll keep a sharp eye on the ripe grapes so no one steals them.

REUBEN: You're a good man, Lamech. I know I can trust you and Enoch with this vineyard while I travel.

LAMECH: Leave everything to me. I'll treat the property as though it were my own.

REUBEN: Good. I'll send someone to collect the harvest. Of course, you and Enoch may keep part of the fruit as payment for your help.

LAMECH: Thank you. Go on your trip and don't worry about a thing. Your vineyard is in good hands.

REUBEN: OK. Good-bye.

(REUBEN *exits rights*.)

LAMECH: Hey, Enoch, come here.

(ENOCH *enters from stage left*.)

ENOCH: Is he gone?

LAMECH: Yeah, he's gone.

ENOCH: Good riddance. He gets to go off on an exciting journey while we kill ourselves working in his vineyard so he can have all the fruit.

LAMECH: He's giving us a share of it.

ENOCH: A drop in the bucket, that's what he's giving us.

LAMECH: We agreed to it, didn't we?

ENOCH: Yeah, but I had my fingers crossed.

LAMECH: You know what?

ENOCH: What?

LAMECH: So did I.

ENOCH: You did?

LAMECH: Yeah. And now that he's gone, we can run this vineyard the way we want to.

ENOCH: Now that sounds right to me.

LAMECH: The first thing we'll do is change the vineyard's layout.

ENOCH: How come? Reuben drew you a picture of exactly how he wanted the rows of grapevines planted.

LAMECH: I know, I know. He told me to plant them six feet apart. Well, I'm going to plant them three feet apart.

ENOCH: That means more work because you'll have to plant more rows of grapevines.

LAMECH: Precisely, my fellow laborer.

ENOCH: You're making no sense.

LAMECH: Reuben thinks there will be a certain number of rows. We won't tell him about the extra rows, and we'll keep all the fruit from those rows for ourselves.

ENOCH: Oh, now I see! We'll be rich!

LAMECH: Well, not rich, but maybe we can save enough money to buy our own vineyards.

ENOCH: I like that idea. I've always wanted to be rolling in the dough, er, grapes.

LAMECH: Let's get busy. Here, take a hoe and we'll start getting the ground ready to plant.

(LAMECH *hands* ENOCH *a hoe and takes one for himself. The two men work their way toward stage right as they pretend to hoe rows. They exit right.*)

Act 2

(In the vineyard with grapevines, LAMECH *and* ENOCH *walk together.)*

LAMECH: These grapes are about ready to harvest.

ENOCH: My back is killing me. Working in this vineyard has been no picnic.

LAMECH: I never said it would be easy.

ENOCH: I think we deserve more payment than we're getting from Reuben, even with the extra grapevine rows he doesn't know about.

LAMECH: I wouldn't mind making some extra money.

ENOCH: The more grape juice and raisins we can make and sell from this harvest, the richer we'll be.

LAMECH: All we have to do is keep Reuben from finding out what a good harvest we're having.

ENOCH: How do we do that?

LAMECH: We can start right now.

ENOCH: How's that?

LAMECH: Do you see that person walking along the road?

*(*LAMECH *points to stage right, where* ISAIAH *enters.)*

ENOCH: Who's that?

LAMECH: I'm not sure, but I'll bet Reuben sent him. Don't tell him how good our harvest is.

ENOCH: OK.

ISAIAH: Hello. You must be Lamech and Enoch.

LAMECH: Yes, we are. And who are you?

ISAIAH: My name is Isaiah. Reuben sent me. He asked me to collect his share of the fruit harvest.

LAMECH: The harvest is just starting, and it doesn't look like it will be a very good one.

ISAIAH: That's strange. Your vines are heavily loaded with grapes, and they look like they've been planted awfully close together. You must have tons and tons of grapes.

LAMECH: Not us. Much of what you see is leaves.

(ISAIAH *reaches down and picks up a vine loaded with grapes.*)

ISAIAH: This looks like a pretty healthy crop to me.

LAMECH: Well, yes, that's, uh, one of our better branches.

ISAIAH: Looks promising to me. Reuben will be glad to get news of such a healthy harvest.

LAMECH: Like I said, it's not as good as it looks.

ISAIAH: Reuben will expect his share of this bountiful crop, and I'm here to collect it. I'll have baskets sent in right away so you can start filling them with Reuben's share.

LAMECH: I don't think so.

ISAIAH: What?

LAMECH: We have other plans for you.

(LAMECH *approaches* ISAIAH *menacingly.*)

ISAIAH: You wouldn't dare mistreat a messenger from this vineyard's owner!

LAMECH: Oh, wouldn't I! Enoch, take him into the store-room at the watchtower and show him we mean business. Maybe he'll take a more "accurate" share of grapes to Reuben then.

ENOCH: With pleasure!

(ENOCH *drags* ISAIAH *by the arm off stage right.*)

LAMECH: That's one messenger indisposed of. I wonder how many more Reuben will send.

(ENOCH *enters right, proudly dusting off his hands.*)

ENOCH: I took care of him! He'll think twice before he ever comes back here to collect grapes.

LAMECH: Good. He'll be too embarrassed to tell Reuben that he failed to collect any harvest. He'll leave the area and never return.

(ENOCH *and* LAMECH *exit right.*)

Act 3

(LAMECH *and* ENOCH *use hoes to weed grapevines at center stage.*)

LAMECH: We're having a bumper crop, Enoch.

ENOCH: I can almost count the money in my pocket when we sell the grape juice and raisins.

LAMECH: Don't count yet. We may have trouble on our hands.

ENOCH: What do you mean?

LAMECH: See those two people walking toward the vineyard?

(LAMECH *points to stage left.*)

ENOCH: Yeah, I see them. Who do you think they are?

LAMECH: More messengers from Reuben.

ENOCH: We can take care of them!

LAMECH: The trick will be to separate them. We can overcome one easier than we can tackle two.

ENOCH: You've got a point.

LAMECH: When they come, you take one of them to the storeroom. While he's looking at what's there, you knock him out. Then come back here and help me overpower the second guy.

ENOCH: Hey, that's my kind of plan!

LAMECH: Quiet. Here they come.

(AMOS *and* MICAH *enter stage left.*)

AMOS: We're looking for Lamech. Do you know where we can find him?

LAMECH: I'm Lamech.

AMOS: Good. I'm Amos, and this is Micah.

MICAH: Reuben sent us to collect the harvest.

LAMECH: Fine. I wondered when Reuben would send someone.

AMOS: He sent a man named Isaiah earlier. But the man never returned.

LAMECH: We never saw an Isaiah here, did we, Enoch?

ENOCH: No one named Isaiah ever came here to collect the harvest.

MICAH: Isaiah was one of Reuben's best workers. It's not like him to disappear.

LAMECH: You know how dangerous traveling on these roads can be.

ENOCH: Bandits everywhere, just waiting to attack.

MICAH: I guess we'll never know what happened to Isaiah.

LAMECH: I'm sorry. But let's concentrate on more pleasant things. Enoch, show Micah the harvest we have in the storeroom while I show Amos around.

ENOCH: I'd be glad to. Come, Micah. I'll give you a tour.

(ENOCH *and* MICAH *exit right.*)

LAMECH: As you can see, Amos, we have a lot of grapes still waiting to be harvested.

AMOS: This is a wonderful harvest. Reuben will be pleased.

LAMECH: Enoch and I have worked very hard to keep weeds away from the vines and to be sure no one steals the harvest.

AMOS: You seem to have an unusual technique.

LAMECH: What do you mean?

AMOS: It looks like the grapevines are very close together.

LAMECH: An optical illusion. The harvest is so great, it make the vines look closer together.

AMOS: Reuben will want to know how you managed to grow such a good harvest.

LAMECH: It's simple. Hard work! We weed the vineyard all the time and hoe the soil around each vine to make it healthier.

AMOS: Excellent. Bring some baskets, and I'll help you pick the grapes. They look ready to harvest.

LAMECH: Uh, well, let me see if I can find some baskets.

(ENOCH *enters right.*)

LAMECH: There you are, Enoch. Did everything go well at the storeroom?

ENOCH: Very well. Micah is still down there. He was so amazed by the harvest there that I think it over-whelmed him. He's waiting there now, if you know what I mean.

LAMECH: Yes. Well, uh, Amos here wants some baskets so he can help us pick grapes.

ENOCH: How nice. I'll see what I can find.

(ENOCH *exits right and immediately returns carrying a straw basket. He quietly sneaks up behind* AMOS, *then shoves the basket over his head.*)

AMOS: What!? Help! Help!!

(LAMECH *and* ENOCH *struggle with* AMOS *until he grows quiet.* ENOCH *takes the basket off* AMOS's *head.*)

LAMECH: Uh-oh. I think we overdid it.

ENOCH: He's not breathing.

LAMECH: No. I think he's dead.

ENOCH: I didn't mean to kill him.

LAMECH: We'd better bury him before anyone discovers the body.

ENOCH: OK.

LAMECH: What shape is Micah in?

ENOCH: He's unconscious. I threw stones at him. One hit him in the head and knocked him out.

LAMECH: We'll bury Amos, then we'll cart Micah away to some remote hillside.

ENOCH: OK.

(ENOCH *and* LAMECH *drag* AMOS *off stage right.*)

Act 4

(ENOCH *and* LAMECH *stand in front of the grapevines a few days later.*)

LAMECH: It's been several days since Amos and Micah came. I wonder if Reuben will send anyone else.

ENOCH: I hope not. We've made lots of grape juice, and we have many grapes lying in the sun, turning into raisins. A few more weeks and we'll be wealthy men.

LAMECH: We can sell the harvest and hop on a camel caravan to some faraway place. Then we'll live the rich life.

ENOCH: I love it!

LAMECH: Oops. Let's not get in to big a hurry.

ENOCH: How's that?

LAMECH: I see someone coming.

(LAMECH *points to stage left.* ENOCH *shades his eyes and looks.*)

ENOCH: I only see one person.

LAMECH: We can take care of him in short order.

ENOCH: Yeah, knock him on the head with a hoe. Whack!

(ENOCH *takes a hoe and demonstrates in the air.*)

LAMECH: Don't get carried away. We don't want to let him know our plan.

ENOCH: Sorry. I got carried away.

(JOSHUA *enters left.*)

LAMECH: Welcome, Stranger. How may I help you?

JOSHUA: I am the son of Reuben, owner of this vineyard.

LAMECH: Welcome! I'm Lamech, and this is Enoch.

JOSHUA: My father has heard distressing stories about this vineyard.

LAMECH: Distressing?

ENOCH: But everything is fine here, as you can see.

JOSHUA: Word has reached my father that his messengers

have been beaten up and killed when they try to collect the harvest.

LAMECH: You must be mistaken. We have seen no messengers.

ENOCH: That's right. No messengers came this way.

JOSHUA: Perhaps they came to the wrong vineyard. At any rate, my father has sent me to collect the harvest. He told me the vineyard tenants would respect me because I am his son.

LAMECH: Of course. We are honored by your presence, Joshua.

ENOCH: Shall I show him the storeroom?

LAMECH: Just point the way, and let him see it for himself.

ENOCH: But. . . .

LAMECH: Let him do as he wishes.

JOSHUA: I will inspect the storeroom—and the rest of the vineyard too—by myself.

LAMECH: Go that way, and you'll come to the storeroom.

(LAMECH *points to stage right.* JOSHUA *exits right.*)

ENOCH: Why did you send him off by himself, Lamech? I was ready to attack him in at the storeroom.

LAMECH: We have to talk.

ENOCH: About what?

LAMECH: About Joshua.

ENOCH: Yeah, we do.

LAMECH: He's the heir to this vineyard.

ENOCH: The heir?

LAMECH: Yeah, you know. He will inherit this vineyard when Reuben decides it's time for him to have it.

ENOCH: Oh, yeah. He'll be the new owner.

LAMECH: If we kill him, we could be the new owners.

ENOCH: How's that?

LAMECH: Without an heir, Reuben will have no one to leave this vineyard to but us.

ENOCH: You think so?

LAMECH: Yes.

ENOCH: Then what are we waiting for? Let's kill Joshua.

LAMECH: We've got to have a good plan, something that will look like an accident.

ENOCH: OK. Let's start planning.

LAMECH: It's got to be good enough to fool Reuben.

(ENOCH *and* LAMECH *exit right as they talk about a plan.*)

Act 5

(ENOCH *and* LAMECH *stand in front of the grapevines, with hoes in their hands.*)

LAMECH: It's done, Enoch. Joshua is dead. The vineyard is ours. No one will find his body at the bottom of that remote well.

ENOCH: You mean we don't have to hop on a camel caravan to a faraway country?

LAMECH: That's right. We can stay here and get richer and richer each year from the harvest of this vineyard.

ENOCH: Don't you think Reuben will send more messengers?

LAMECH: This vineyard is too much trouble for him. He'll never come back here now.

ENOCH: Then, let's celebrate.

LAMECH: First, let's finish getting in the harvest. Then we can celebrate.

ENOCH: You're a slave driver.

LAMECH: It's only for a few more days, till the harvest is over. Then we can live it up.

ENOCH: I'm ready for that!

(LAMECH *puts his hand over his eyes and gazes toward left.*)

ENOCH: What's the matter?

LAMECH: I thought I saw something.

(ENOCH *shades his eyes and also looks toward stage left.*)

ENOCH: Someone's coming.

LAMECH: Oh, no. Another messenger?

ENOCH: Couldn't be another of Reuben's sons. I think he only had one.

LAMECH: It isn't a messenger.

ENOCH: That's a relief. Who is it?

LAMECH: It's Reuben!

ENOCH: Oh, no. We've got to hide. He'll kill us if he finds out what we've done.

LAMECH: Don't panic. We'll hide, but we'll do it so it doesn't look like we're hiding.

ENOCH: Huh?

LAMECH: We'll get behind these grapevines and pretend to be hoeing. Maybe Reuben won't see us.

ENOCH: OK, but I don't think it's going to work.

(LAMECH *and* ENOCH *take their hoes and hide behind the grapevines at center stage.* REUBEN *enters stage left.*)

REUBEN: Lamech! Where are you?

(LAMECH *and* ENOCH *stand very still behind the grapevines.*)

REUBEN: Lamech! I know you're here. Come out. Now!

ENOCH: I think you'd better go.

LAMECH: Shhh!

REUBEN: Aha! I see you behind those grapevines.

(REUBEN *heads toward the vines.* LAMECH *and* ENOCH *step out into the open.*)

LAMECH: Oh, Reuben! Hello. We were so busy working among the vines that we didn't hear you.

REUBEN: Didn't you hear my messengers or my son either?

ENOCH: Messengers? Son?

REUBEN: Yes. I sent three messengers, and then I sent my son to collect the harvest. My son and a messenger were killed and the other two were badly hurt.

LAMECH: I'm sorry to hear that.

REUBEN: You know what I'm talking about.

ENOCH: No, we don't.

REUBEN: Yes, you do, and so do the villagers around here. They told me what happened.

LAMECH: Surely, you wouldn't believe the villagers. They're jealous of us for having these good jobs.

REUBEN: The town leader himself told me. He's a wealthy man and has no reason to be jealous or to lie.

(ENOCH *throws down his hoe, kneels and clutches* REUBEN'S *knees.*)

ENOCH: Have mercy! It's true, it's true. We are ignorant men who didn't know any better. Please forgive us.

LAMECH: Be quiet, Enoch! Reuben, he doesn't know what he's talking about. He's gotten this way from overwork.

ENOCH: I tried to stop him, but Lamech wanted to kill everyone.

LAMECH: See what I mean? He's having a nervous breakdown. Nothing he says makes sense.

(REUBEN *pushes* ENOCH *away.* ENOCH *stands cowering behind* LAMECH.)

REUBEN: You're both lying, thieving tenants who wanted what wasn't yours. You had very good jobs here and were well-cared for.

LAMECH: All right, we admit it. We wanted to own the vineyard. We thought we could have it if we did away with your messengers and your son.

REUBEN: My vineyard is big enough to provide a good living for many workers. I always take care of my employees, because I care about them. But you have betrayed me, so you can no longer work here.

ENOCH: Please don't throw us out.

REUBEN: You're on your own now. Get out of my sight.

ENOCH: But this is our home!

REUBEN: There is no place here for people who lie, steal, and kill. My messengers and my son came to help you collect the harvest, but you had no respect for them. When you rejected them, you rejected me, too. Now I am turning you away. Go!

LAMECH: OK, we'll go.

ENOCH: Where will we go?

LAMECH: Shut up and follow me.

ENOCH: Following you gets me into nothing but trouble.

LAMECH: Don't blame me. You got a lot of pleasure from hurting those people.

ENOCH: If you don't watch out, I'll teach you a lesson, too.

LAMECH: Come on, let's go. You walk in front.

(LAMECH *pushes* ENOCH *in front of him. They exit right.*)

REUBEN: I will find people willing to harvest this fruit, and I will put them in charge of this vineyard. There must be someone willing to do the work that needs to be done. The hardest part of my job is finding willing workers. I'll just have to keep looking until I find them.

(REUBEN *exits left.*)

15 The Hidden Treasure
Based on Matthew 13:44

(the value of God's kingdom)

CHARACTERS

SAM
JIM
TOM, the store manager

PROPS

Several toys and shelves to resemble a toy store
An old train
Fake snake
Wheelbarrow full of toys
Toy bulldozer
Squirt gun
Bright colored bandanna

Act 1

(On a sidewalk outside a toy store. SAM and JIM talk together at center front. Behind them in center of stage are several shelves containing toys.)

JIM: Hey, Sam, have you decided what you want for your birthday yet?

SAM: No. I haven't found anything that really interests me.

JIM: I wish you'd hurry up and think of something. Your birthday's next week, and I still don't know what you want for a present.

SAM: Get me something you want. I'll like it. You know what everyone says about us—we're so alike we could be brothers.

JIM: I know, but I still want to get you what *you* want.

SAM: Don't worry. I'll like whatever you get me.

JIM: Have you been in this toy store yet?

(JIM *points to the toy store on stage.*)

SAM: No.

JIM: Let's go in. You might find something there.

SAM: OK, but I've been to so many toy stores, I'm sick of them.

(JIM *and* SAM *walk into the toy store and begin looking at toys on the shelves.*)

JIM: Hey, look at this. It's a little bulldozer.

SAM: I've already got one.

JIM: How about this toy snake? You could scare all the girls with it.

SAM: I have one of those, too.

JIM: Then, how about this squirt gun? Everyone needs two or three squirt guns.

SAM: Not me.

JIM: Boy, you sure are hard to shop for.

SAM: Sorry. I told you I'd like whatever you got me.

JIM: You're driving me nuts.

SAM: I said I was sorry.

JIM: Maybe I'll get you a gift certificate so you can drive yourself crazy trying to find something you want.

SAM: Good. Then you'll stop driving *me* crazy with all your questions.

JIM: You mean you really want a gift certificate?

SAM: I guess so.

JIM: OK, I'll get you one, if I can find the shopkeeper.

(*As* SAM *looks through the shelves, he finds a train and becomes very excited.*)

SAM: Jim! Look at this!

JIM: What?

SAM: This train.

JIM: Looks pretty old to me, like it was somebody's toy a long time ago.

SAM: It's what I've been looking for, Jim. This is the present I want.

JIM: I can't buy you that. All I've got is a dollar.

SAM: I don't care how much this train costs. It's what I want. I'll empty my bank, I'll sell my jet fighter plane. I'll sell every toy I have to get this train.

JIM: You're really crazy.

SAM: Have you ever wanted anything so badly you just had to have it?

JIM: Not enough to sell everything I have.

SAM: Then you can't understand how I feel.

JIM: I guess not. But you're my friend, and I'll do what I can to help you.

SAM: Thanks.

JIM: The first thing we need to know is how much it costs.

(SAM *picks up the engine and looks underneath it.*)

SAM: I don't see a price tag.

(TOM *enters from stage center back.*)

TOM: Can I help you boys.

SAM: How much is this train? I really want to buy it.

JIM: Just a minute, Sam. Excuse me, Sir. Sam and I need to talk in private.

(JIM *grabs* SAM's *arm and starts pulling him toward the front of the stage.*)

SAM: Cut it out! I'm trying to talk to the store manager.

JIM: You can do that in a minute. First, we need to talk.

SAM: OK, OK. Excuse me, Sir. We'll be right back.

(JIM *drags* SAM *out of the store to front stage center.*)

SAM: You'd better have a good reason for dragging me out of that store after I finally found what I wanted.

JIM: That's what we need to talk about.

SAM: You dragged me out here to talk about that train?

JIM: No!

SAM: What, then?

JIM: To talk about how you're going to get it.

SAM: I'm going to buy it, that's how I'm going to get it.

JIM: I know, I know. But how much are you going to pay for it?

SAM: That's what I was trying to find out when you dragged me out here.

JIM: I dragged you out because you don't know when to stop.

SAM: When to stop? What are you talking about?

JIM: I can see you don't have the faintest idea of how to bargain.

SAM: I don't want to bargain. I want to buy that train.

JIM: I think he will come down on his price if you bargain right.

SAM: Oh, yeah?

JIM: Yeah. All you've got to do is act like you don't really want the train.

SAM: But I do want it.

JIM: I know. Your face lit up like a spotlight when you saw it.

SAM: So?

JIM: So you've got to play it cool. Pretend you don't care about that train. Do you want to learn how to bargain for that train or not?

SAM: I guess so, if it means I can afford to buy it.

JIM: That's more like it. When we walk back into the store, you let me do the talking.

SAM: OK, I guess.

(SAM *and* JIM *walk back into the store.* TOM *stands behind one of the shelves, looking slightly amused.*)

TOM: Can I help you boys find something?

SAM: I've already found it.

JIM: *(Whispers)* Shhh! I'll do the talking, remember?

SAM: *(Whispers)* OK, OK.

TOM: Excuse me. I didn't hear that.

JIM: We were just getting ready to leave.

SAM: No!

TOM: You can look around as long as you want.

JIM: Well, we might spend another minute or two here, but we must leave soon for an important engagement.

SAM: *(Whispers)* What engagement?

JIM: *(Whispers)* The one at the brain surgeon's to get your head examined. Keep quiet and let me do the talking!

SAM: *(Whispers)* If you make me lose that train, you'll be in big trouble.

JIM: *(Whispers)* Relax. I know what I'm doing.

TOM: Do you boys have laryngitis or something? You're doing an awful lot of whispering.

JIM: Sorry. We just had an important private matter to discuss.

TOM: If you see anything you're interested in, let me know.

SAM: Wait.

JIM: *(Whispers)* Hush!

TOM: You're whispering again.

JIM: There are a couple of things we're interested in.

TOM: Yes?

JIM: The bulldozer over here. How much is it?

TOM: Five dollars.

JIM: That's a little steep.

TOM: It's very sturdy.

JIM: How about the squirt gun?

TOM: You can have it for fifty cents.

JIM: Fifty cents, huh?

TOM: That's right.

JIM: How about this train?

SAM: Yes, how about this train?

JIM: *(Whispers)* Be quiet!

TOM: I put the train out for display. It's really not for sale.

SAM: Not for sale?

TOM: No. It belonged to me when I was a child. It's almost an antique.

JIM: It does look a little old and scuffed up.

SAM: It's beautiful!

JIM: *(Whispers)* I told you to be quiet!

TOM: Thanks. I always liked that train.

SAM: Would you consider selling it?

JIM: *(Whispers)* I can see you're not interested in bargaining! I'll wait for you outside.

(JIM *stalks huffily out of the store and exits stage right.*)

TOM: I might sell it, but it would have to be to the right person.

SAM: I'd like to have it more than anything.

TOM: More than anything?

SAM: Yes, Sir!

TOM: What would you give me for that train?

SAM: Well, I've got ten dollars in my bank.

(TOM *gently shakes his head.*)

SAM: And I've got lots of toys I could give you. There's my fancy new jet fighter plane and my fire truck. Then I have a teddy bear that plays Christmas songs. Aunt Mildred gave it to me—she forgets I'm a big kid now. And I've got a whole toy box full of other things I'd give you in exchange for that train.

TOM: A whole toy box full?

SAM: That's right.

TOM: You mean you'd give me all your toys for that train?

SAM: Everything. As soon as I saw that train, I knew it was what I wanted.

TOM: What's your name, son?

SAM: Sam.

TOM: Well, Sam, that train was my favorite toy when I was a boy. I'm not sure I want to give it up.

SAM: Besides giving you the ten dollars in my bank and all my toys, I'll clean up your store for a whole month. I'll be here every day after school to sweep and take out the trash, and I'll even mop the floor and wash your windows.

TOM: You'd do all that to get this train?

SAM: Yes, Sir. It's what I've always wanted. I've been looking real hard for a birthday present, but I couldn't find what I wanted until I saw that train.

TOM: Well, Sam, if the train means so much to you, then you're the person who should be the owner.

SAM: Thanks!

TOM: If you get your parents' permission to give away all your toys and spend the ten dollars in your bank to buy this train, you can have it. You won't have to sweep or mop or wash windows.

SAM: Thanks a lot! I'll talk to my parents. If they say it's OK to give you my toys, I'll be back tomorrow.

(SAM *races out of the store. As he walks out the door,* JIM *enters from stage right.*)

JIM: Well, did you get the train?

SAM: Not yet. First, I have to ask my parents if I can give the manager ten dollars and all my toys.

JIM: You're a nut!

SAM: Maybe, but I love that train.

JIM: I told you if you let me do the talking, you could get that train at a cheaper price.

SAM: I can afford the train.

JIM: But you have to give up all you've got.

SAM: It's worth it. I want that train more than I've ever wanted anything.

JIM: It's your money and your toys, but I still think you're crazy.

SAM: I'm going to ask my parents about buying the train. Want to come?

JIM: Sure. I wouldn't miss this show for the world.

(SAM *and* JIM *exit stage right.*)

Act 2

(In front of the toy store. SAM *enters pushing a wheelbarrow full of toys.* JIM *follows, shaking his head.)*

JIM: I didn't think you'd go through with it, Sam. You're dumber than I thought.

SAM: I've heard enough of your opinions about me. These are my toys, and I can do what I want with them. My parents gave me permission to trade them for the train, so get lost.

JIM: OK, OK. But I never thought they'd agree. They didn't even get mad.

(SAM *pushes the wheelbarrow into the store.* TOM *enters from center back.*)

TOM: You brought all your toys?

SAM: And my ten dollars.

JIM: But he forgot his brains.

SAM: Hush.

TOM: Your friend doesn't like the trade we're making?

SAM: He thinks I'm crazy.

TOM: Well, there's something your friend doesn't know.

JIM: What's that?

SAM: There's a lot of things my friend doesn't know. And one of them is when to keep quiet.

TOM: It's OK. Your friend doesn't understand what it's like to want something so badly you will give up everything for it.

JIM: You've got *that* right.

TOM: I wouldn't have let you have this train if you weren't willing to give up everything you had for it.

SAM: You wouldn't?

TOM: That's right.

JIM: How come?

TOM: Because that train was my favorite toy when I was a child. I remember the day my father brought it home, all wrapped up in a big box. He knew how much I wanted a train, so he spent the money he needed for a coat to buy me that train. My father sacrificed a great deal to give me the train. I want someone to have it who will take care of it and love it the way I did.

SAM: Your father must have loved you very much to go without a coat so you could have this train.

TOM: He did. He made lots of sacrifices for me. And now that I see you have sacrificed your money and your toys to buy this train, I know you are the person the train should belong to.

(JIM *reaches into his pocket and pulls out a brightly colored bandanna. He blows his noise loudly on it.*)

JIM: That's a neat story.

SAM: Do you still think I'm crazy?

JIM: No. You're smart, real smart.

SAM: I'm not smart, just happy to get what I really want.

TOM: And wise to know its worth.

JIM: Yeah? What's it worth?

TOM: In dollars, probably not much. But in love and in happy memories, it's worth a great deal.

SAM: Help me unload these toys, Jim, so I can take my train home.

JIM: OK.

(JIM *and* SAM *quickly unload the wheelbarrow, while* SAM *ad libs about some of the toys he puts on the store shelf. He might say something like this: I got this plane on my sixth birthday. When I was two, I took the wheel off this truck and flushed it down the toilet.*)

TOM: Now that you've unloaded the toys, let me put the train in your wheelbarrow.

(TOM *carefully loads the train into the wheelbarrow.*)

TOM: I know it's going to a good home.
SAM: I'll take real good care of it, I promise.
JIM: Bye.
TOM: Good-bye.

(SAM *pushes the wheelbarrow off stage right while* JIM *follows.*)

TOM: I know that boy will take care of my train, because he was willing to give up everything he had to buy it.

(TOM *exits center back.*)